W9-CGK-925

The
Fast Forward
MBA in Business
Communication

THE FAST FORWARD MBA SERIES

The Fast Forward MBA Series provides time-pressed business professionals and students with concise, one-stop information to help them solve business problems and make smart, informed business decisions. All of the volumes, written by industry leaders, contain "tough ideas made easy." The published books in this series are:

The Fast Forward MBA in Negotiating & Dealmaking
(0-471-25698-6)
by Roy J. Lewicki and Alexander Hiam

The Fast Forward MBA in Financial Planning
(0-471-23829-5)
by Ed McCarthy

The Fast Forward MBA in Hiring
(0-471-24212-8)
by Max Messmer

The Fast Forward MBA in Investing
(0-471-24661-1)
by Jack Waggoner

The Fast Forward MBA in Technology Management
(0-471-23980-1)
by Daniel J. Petrozzo

The Fast Forward MBA Pocket Reference
(0-471-14595-5)
by Paul A. Argenti

The Fast Forward MBA in Marketing
(0-471-16616-2)
by Dallas Murphy

The Fast Forward MBA in Business
(0-471-14660-9)
by Virginia O'Brien

The Fast Forward MBA in Finance
(0-471-10930-4)
by John Tracy

The Fast Forward MBA in Project Management
(0-471-32546-5)
by Eric Verzuh

The Fast Forward MBA in Business Communication

LAUREN VICKER
RON HEIN

John Wiley & Sons, Inc.

New York • Chichester • Weinheim • Brisbane • Singapore • Toronto

This book is printed on acid-free paper. ∞

Copyright © 1999 by Lauren Vicker & Ron Hein. All rights reserved.

Published by John Wiley & Sons, Inc.
Published simultaneously in Canada.

No part of this publication may be reproduced, stored in a retrieval system or transmitted in any form or by any means, electronic, mechanical, photocopying, recording, scanning or otherwise, except as permitted under Sections 107 or 108 of the 1976 United States Copyright Act, without either the prior written permission of the Publisher, or authorization through payment of the appropriate per-copy fee to the Copyright Clearance Center, 222 Rosewood Drive, Danvers, MA 01923, (978) 750-8400, fax (978) 750-4744. Requests to the Publisher for permission should be addressed to the Permissions Department, John Wiley & Sons, Inc., 605 Third Avenue, New York, NY 10158-0012, (212) 850-6011, fax (212) 850-6008, E-Mail: PERMREQ@WILEY.COM.

This publication is designed to provide accurate and authoritative information in regard to the subject matter covered. It is sold with the understanding that the publisher is not engaged in rendering professional services. If legal, accounting, medical, psychological or any other expert assistance is required, the ser-vices of a competent professional person should be sought.

Library of Congress Cataloging-in-Publication Data:
Vicker, Lauren.
   The fast forward MBA in business communication / Lauren Vicker, Ron Hein.
      p.   cm. — (The fast forward MBA series)
   Includes bibliographical references and index.
   ISBN 0-471-32731-X (pbk. : alk. paper)
   1. Business communication. I. Hein, Ron. II. Title.
   III. Series
   HF5718.V53   1999   99-19466
   658.4'5—dc21   CIP

Printed in the United States of America.

10   9   8   7   6   5   4   3   2   1

Lauren Vicker is a Professor and Chair of the Communication/Journalism Department of St. John Fisher College. Vicker taught for seven years at the Simon School of Business at the University of Rochester. In addition to teaching, Vicker offers presentation skills training to professional and academic groups on a consulting basis. She lives in Penfield, New York. Lauren Vicker can be reached at vicker@sjfc.edu.

Ron Hein is president of Ron Hein & Associates, Inc., a corporation that provides writing, editing, and consulting services to individuals and clients such as Xerox and Eastman Kodak. He also taught in the full-time MBA program at the Simon School of Business, University of Rochester, for seven years and continues to teach in its Executive Development MBA program. He lives in Webster, New York. Ron Hein can be reached at ron@eznet.net or ron-hein.com.

ACKNOWLEDGMENTS

I would like to thank Dr. David Arnold and Dr. Jim Seward of St. John Fisher College for supporting the sabbatical leave that gave me time to work on this book. I also owe thanks to those who contributed ideas and material, including Jim Vicker, Judy Isserlis, Eric Skopec, Nic Marinaccio, Peter Monk, Dennis Garrett, Alex Ryan, and all the students at Fisher and the Simon School who have taught me so much over the years. A special thanks to Fisher student Michael Leaver, who kept me organized in the office and was always willing to read, edit, copy, and FedEx files with great enthusiasm and a positive attitude. And finally, thanks to Jim, Matt, and Chrissie for their unconditional support and understanding while I was involved with this project.
—Lauren Vicker

I would like to acknowledge the support of my family, friends, and colleagues. Specifically, I would like to thank the following: Lauren Vicker for her willingness to understand that medical problems sometimes preclude efficiency. Tammany Kramer for her willingness to work with me over the last five years, and for her insights and intuitive ability to see things clearly. Deb Beckmann-Hein and my daughter, Lindsay Beckmann-Hein, who continually listen to my musings, help me clarify my thinking, and make certain that I set family-centered priorities. My many friends, students and clients who have helped me understand that it is important to use systematic processes that lead to win-win options. . . . and to those who seek to continually improve themselves and their world.
—Ron Hein

Finally, we offer our deepest gratitude to our editor Renana Meyers, whose enthusiasm was infectious, whose support was unconditional, and whose patience seemed endless.

CONTENTS

CONTENTS

CONTENTS

Welcome to *The Fast Forward MBA in Business Communication.* We hope you have opened this book because you know that successful managers and executives use effective oral and written communication skills to get the results they need.

The Fast Forward MBA in Business Communication is different from other business books on writing and presentations. This book will offer you the following:

- Concise content, logically organized and practically oriented
- A user-friendly format that allows you to read the entire book or selected parts
- An organized process approach to both business writing and business presentations
- Links to strategic management communication and sound management perspectives

The Fast Forward MBA in Business Communication is guaranteed to save you time and money. Managers and executives frequently waste considerable time by using faulty processes for documents and presentations. A systematic process would enable them to work more efficiently, eliminate redundancy, and communicate their ideas more effectively. The tools in this book provide you with such a process.

Many business executives pick up a book like this because they wish to improve their individual skills in writing or presentations or both. Others need tips to help their team members work more effectively. This book will help you with both perspectives.

We cover the individual writing process in detail in Part 2, including the following topics:

- Writing and editing processes
- Organizing the logic and structure of your document
- Developing the layout and design of your document
- Preparing different types of documents:
  Memos
  E-mail

Proposals and requests for proposals

Reports

The individual presentation process is presented in Part 3. The topics include the following:

- Defining your purpose
- Analyzing your audience
- Gathering supporting materials
- Organizing your ideas
- Planning visual support
- Improving delivery skills
- Handling the question-and-answer session
- Dealing with speech anxiety

In addition to business writing and business presentations, we include two additional and important perspectives.

In Part 1, we discuss strategic management communication and its relationship to business communication. Rather than viewing business communication solely as the purview of a single individual, businesses today are adopting more of a companywide perspective. The explosion of information and information technology has mandated that companies find ways to organize their documents, to share information between and among individuals and workgroups, and to make effective use of communication resources to enhance the value of oral and written messages. We address companywide strategies that will eliminate time currently spent producing unused and unneeded documents and presentations, and we focus on improving skills, processes, and products.

In Part 4, we discuss strategies for writing and presenting as a team. These guidelines are significant for individuals in many companies that emphasize teams and workgroups as the primary vehicle for accomplishing tasks. The ability to work successfully with others is often a major factor in determining the success of a document or a presentation as a persuasive communication tool.

We also provide appendixes with supplementary materials, including a Self-Diagnostic Grammar Test and Guidelines for Special Occasion Presentations. Our web site (ron-hein.com), contains additional sample materials that demonstrate how to design documents and visuals for maximum impact.

According to Anne Fisher of *Fortune* magazine, a survey of the 1,000 largest employers in the United States revealed that 96 percent maintain that employees must have good communication skills in order to get ahead.[1] We know you believe communication skills are important, because you've opened this book. We hope that you will find it to be an excellent resource guide for developing and refining your communication skills as you advance in your business career. We welcome your questions, comments, and feedback at our web site (ron-hein.com). And we guarantee that improved business writing and business presentation skills will save you time and money.

Stellar Performer:
Department of Mathematical
Science, University of Delaware

Business communication is a topic that cuts across all professions and fields, and the recognition of effective communication skills as an integral business tool is becoming more widespread. Twenty years ago, for example, accountants were required only to crunch numbers and spent little time interacting with clients. Today, accountants routinely make presentations, interview clients, and write proposals. Indeed, it would be difficult to find a professional position today where oral and written communication skills are unimportant.

One of the more recent, and perhaps surprising, entries into the communication skills camp has come from the field of mathematics. Professors at the University of Delaware's Department of Mathematical Science have incorporated training in presentation skills as part of a major grant funded by the National Science Foundation (NSF). The grant is intended to help graduate students in mathematics make the transition to jobs in business and industry, and part of that transition involves being able to explain their often complex field to others.

"We recognized that, while our graduate students were good at teaching undergraduate courses, they didn't have many good role models in the field for nontechnical presentations," says Delaware mathematics Professor Peter Monk. "Graduate students go to professional conferences and see mathematicians reading their papers, talking to the chalkboard, and not really connecting with the audience." Encouraged by a report from the Society for Industrial and Applied Mathematics, which maintained that "communication is simply too important to be ignored . . . [and] writing and speaking skills are important for all mathematicians . . . ,"[2] the department included a presentation skills seminar in its grant proposal for NSF. In the first year of the grant, seven graduate students and two faculty members participated in the three-day seminar, which provided time for individual presentations and evaluation as well as for discussion of some aspects of presentations particular to the field. On the last day, participants delivered math-related presentations that they had designed for a nonmath audience. "That's something very difficult for us to do," says Dr. Monk. "We're used to talking to other mathematicians, and some complex ideas don't translate well into lay terms. On the other hand, in the business world, you have to be able to explain your ideas and proposals to the people who control your budget."

The commitment at the University of Delaware to incorporating communication skills training into its graduate program in mathematics is a pioneering effort. It is likely that other technical fields will follow the lead of graduate business schools, which now routinely require business writing and business presentations courses as part of their MBA programs. With the globalization of the workforce and the use of multiskilled teams in many corporations today, the need for effective communication skills in every part of an organization will be expected to increase.

The
Fast Forward
MBA in Business
Communication

PART 1

Communication Strategy

Effective business communication is more than the ability of an individual to create a clear memo, a useful executive summary, a good report, or a persuasive presentation. It is a set of individual skills, team or group decisions, *and* company-supported policies, philosophies, and actions that promote the linkage of individuals and groups within an organization. Such linkages ensure that key strategic and operational information is shared appropriately and effectively. Managers and companies that do not develop and encourage the use of such processes give up potential competitive advantages and may under-utilize company strengths.

It is clear that profound changes are occurring in the way that businesses are both doing business and communicating. In Part 1 of this book, we highlight two areas of change:

- Strategic business communication (Chapter 1)
- Document management (Chapter 2)

Changes are occurring in what is being communicated within and outside of organizations, why it is being communicated, and who is doing the communicating. Having closely held information within groups (departments) and not sharing that information was once commonly viewed as appropriate and in the best interest of a company.

Now, companies seek to eliminate those barriers because of necessity.

Managers need to build teams, share information, and appropriately delegate authority to facilitate the completion of projects. A supply-chain view of a corporation, its suppliers, and customers is now accepted and widely implemented as part of an integrated resource management approach.

Managers who keep information private and closely guarded are obstacles to teamwork and to reaching common, companywide goals. Managers who do not accept input from others within and outside of their groups risk failing to identify and solidify critical connections that will make the company fast and innovative.

More than ever, businesses need to promote communication skills to facilitate quick and precise decision making that keeps them competitive. To promote communication skills, it is necessary to focus on companywide perspectives (policies and support), implementation by teams and groups, and the skills of individual contributors. Our goal is to help facilitate that competitive advantage.

CHAPTER 1

Strategic Business Communication

One of the problems facing most businesses is how to keep up with internal and external change. This includes changes in business communication strategies and requirements.

WHAT IS DRIVING CHANGES IN BUSINESS COMMUNICATION?

The need for improved business communication strategies is being driven by the fast demands of business, globalization, and the technology revolution, as well as leadership challenges that require improved business communication strategies and skills at company, team or group, and individual levels.

As shown in Figures 1.1 and 1.2, changes in strategy need to be viewed from three perspectives: companywide, group or team, and individual contributors. Options available are both constrained and enhanced by decisions made at each of those levels. For example, if a company decides to implement a document life-cycle management strategy (Chapter 2) or a document management system, to offer training to employees in communication skills, to use project management systems, to teach effective writing and editing skills (Chapter 3), or to make persuasive presentations, the entire capacity of a company will be enhanced.

New communication strategies have become necessary as a result of the rise of several movements:

- The quality movement pioneered by Deming[1]
- The implementation of integrated supply chains[2,3]

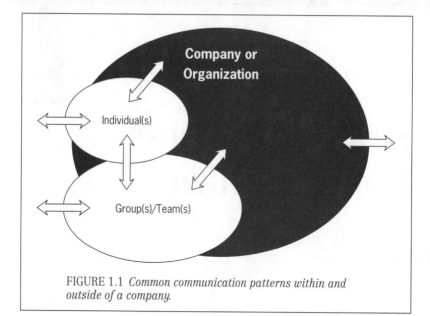

FIGURE 1.1 *Common communication patterns within and outside of a company.*

- The advent of integrated resource management[4]

These initiatives forced a new and improved kind of communication and leadership, as evidenced in the following (see Figure 1.3):

- ISO 9000 standards (www.iso.ch/)
- The Malcolm Baldrige National Quality Awards in the United States (www.quality.nist.gov/)
- The growing use of standards and benchmarks throughout industry and in other areas

Technology has placed new demands on us to order and make sense of data—making effective communication a priority. This means that information (data) must be collected and assembled into databases that can be queried so that computerized systems for tracking and analyzing all aspects of a company become a reality, not a pie-in-the-sky idea. Management groups must work with information systems that link data, facilitate analysis, generate query-based reports, and expedite decision processes if they are to sustain a competitive advantage.

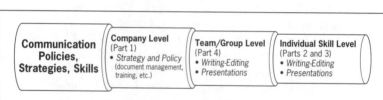

FIGURE 1.2 *Effective business communication depends on a series of interrelated policies, strategies, and skills at the company, team, and individual levels.*

FIGURE 1.3 *Communication strategies and skills are central to multiple business initiatives and requirements.*

BENCHMARKING AND TEAMWORK REQUIRE EXCELLENT COMMUNICATION

In Thomas Kayser's *Mining Group Gold,*[5] in Michael Hammer and James Champy's *Reengineering the Corporation,*[6] and in Robert Camp's insights on benchmarking, the authors make it clear that successful managers and companies effectively share goals, strategies, and other pertinent information.

William Russell indicates that integrated resource management requires that everyone in an organization understand the terminology of other functions—and the impact of those functions on his or her own area. In addition Russell notes that individuals need to understand how the decisions in their own areas will affect other areas. These are all communication issues. Peter Drucker,[7] arguably the "founder" of modern-day management, in his work on manufacturing makes parallel points.

Russell and the American Production and Inventory Control Society (APICS) note that surveys of the most successful companies show that "improving communications between management and workers" is the number one activity those companies are pursuing.

Companies need to know how to share information successfully by using multiple tools (one-on-one meetings, phone calls, e-mail, memos, reports, group meetings, and presentations), which are often dependent on the skills of individual contributors.

In addition, to win a Baldrige award or comply with ISO 9000 requirements, effective internal and external communication processes are needed. Support for this idea can be seen in the work of pioneering thinker

Robert Camp, who examines benchmarking leadership and management processes, the leadership focus of the Baldrige requirements, and the manner in which supply-chain management is implemented in companies such as Xerox, Westinghouse, Texas Instruments, the Ritz-Carlton Hotels, and others.

LEADERSHIP AND NEGOTIATIONS REQUIRE EXCELLENT COMMUNICATION SKILLS

The era of the information age and the demand of the New Economy require extraordinary leadership and negotiation skills—in other words, excellent communication skills. As Stephen Covey writes in *Principle-Centered Leadership,*[8] and as the work of Fisher, Ury, and Patton, *Getting to Yes*[9] suggests, successful negotiations implicitly acknowledge the need for managers and other leaders to communicate well.

Companywide, Team, and Individual Perspectives

The success of individuals, teams, and companies is becoming increasingly dependent on effective business communication because of the the growing complexity of business transactions, products, and services. It is quite common for one company to provide services and products to other companies that are located at some distance. Equally true, more companies need to manage internal information across multiple business locations, locations that are often global. Each of these tasks requires effective communication processes that will decrease transaction and data-sharing time and costs. Because specific barriers—and solutions—to business communication can exist at multiple levels in an organization, answers to the following three broad questions will help to identify communication concerns, potential strengths, and weaknesses or barriers:

- Why should a company use a companywide approach to improve business communication, and specifically, what can a company do?
- How can a workgroup or team improve business communication on specific projects?
- How can individual contributors improve business documents and presentations, as well as related processes and personal skill sets?

For example, if a manager can spend less time creating a proposal that is clearer and more useful, and a senior executive can evaluate it without requesting further data or clarifications, companies should be able to make decisions more rapidly and with greater accuracy. The issue then becomes, what can a company do to make certain that managerial time is not wasted producing and/or using ineffective documents and presentations?

DECIDING YOUR COMMUNICATION STRATEGY

Company-Level Decisions

Communication issues cut across all levels of a business, and key decisions need to be made at different levels. For example, at a company level, decisions might include the following:

- Should our company design and implement databases to support projects that need to be coordinated across various workgroups?

- Would it be cost-effective to develop and use standard formats for internal reports and/or proposals?

- At what point and in which documents or presentations do we support or require the use of color?

- Can we gain efficiencies by standardizing our word processing and presentation software? Should we use Lotus Notes to share information, or should we use Microsoft Word? Should we adopt and support a presentation package (for example, PowerPoint) on a companywide basis, or should we support department-by-department use of whichever presentation package a current manager prefers?

- What are the costs and benefits of providing staff training to improve writing skills or document development processes? What do we train them to do? To what degree of proficiency do we train users?

- Should we install and support voice recognition software for managers who earn $100,000+ a year and type by the hunt-and-peck method?

- What are the costs and benefits of installing an intranet (internal computer network) to share data, documentation, and other information? Which software packages allow documents to be shared (or imported and exported to other packages) with ease and security?

- Should we adopt a document management system (for example, Xerox's DocuShare) so that we can share documents within our company and with outside customers, vendors, and/or consultants?

Team-Level Decisions

At the team or workgroup level, decisions at the level of a specific project can be resolved, often dependent upon the company-level supports that are or are not available. Pertinent decisions include the following:

- Do we use project management concepts (timelines, Gantt charts, PERT charts) for a specific project? Do we use manual or software-based solutions?

- Do we send out a report, or do we make a formal project presentation and provide a report? Do we distribute the report or presentation electronically or as hard copy? What are the advantages, the disadvantages, and the barriers?

- If we do a presentation in person, do we use overheads or a computer-controlled presentation? Can we benefit from real-time access to databases, spreadsheets, and what-if calculations?

- Which team member would be the best presenter, or do we use a team of presenters?

- Which team member will edit the final report or proposal, or do we hire a professional editor?

Individual Decisions

There are also decisions that an individual contributor needs to make, taking into consideration the restrictions of specific work environments and the guidance of managers. Decisions at this level include the following issues:

- Do I use a writing and editing process in order to be more effective and efficient?

- Would it be valuable to use tables to display key information in a report, or is it okay or better to leave it as several paragraphs of text?

- Should I ask a colleague to proofread the materials?

- Do I need to improve my basic grammar skills, or is the 40 to 50 percent accuracy rate of my word processor sufficient?

- Do I need to use a computer-projected presentation, or would overheads or handouts be best, or would just talking with no visual aids be best?

 **IMPLEMENTING YOUR COMMUNICATIONS STRATEGY**

As you can see, these issues are not discrete; they overlap among individuals and groups within a company. That's one reason that business communication issues need to be raised and answered: They are broad issues with very positive or negative effects on individual careers, the outcome of specific projects, and the overall efficiency and profitability of a company.

Evaluating an individual's ability to write, edit, and present information is critical but not sufficient. To improve business communication, specific requirements, strengths, and barriers must be identified and handled at all levels.

The current literature on business communication seldom addresses these issues, and it fails to identify processes that can be used to resolve them. Further, the connection of these issues to leadership and management is not addressed. As a result, individuals and teams are often unable to identify strengths, weaknesses, or barriers, and they cannot get the resources they need to improve business communication and increase efficiency and effectiveness.

Developing Effective Business Communication within a Company or Organization

It is important to complete the following steps at a company level:

- Identify internal and external requirements for communication (documents and presentations).
- Identify resources/strengths.
- Identify barriers (process, personal skills, interpersonal, hardware, software, standards, etc.).
- Develop and implement processes that will eliminate or decrease the barriers.
- Determine the type of support (for example, hardware/software/networks) that can be useful.
- Establish/adopt templates/standards for documents and presentations.
- Determine what training support is needed to increase effectiveness and meet requirements.

COMPANY-LEVEL BUSINESS COMMUNICATION TRENDS

A number of key trends have been emerging in business communication. E-mail is now a staple in the business world, and companies need to address and continually reassess the extent to which to they use the Internet (World Wide Web) for advertising, marketing, research, and document sharing. Beyond the Internet, whether to use intranets is also a key business communication decision. Sophisticated document management systems that use both the Internet and intranets are allowing companies to move closer to, if not paperless offices, offices that can create and share electronic versions of documents easily and securely.

E-mail

Many company-level policy decisions (including software, networks/hardware, and training/support) impact the extent to which e-mail is successfully used. In Chapter 6, we offer suggestions on how to create more functional, useful e-mail messages—literally billions of e-mail messages are sent on a daily basis—and we also review commonly accepted ways to improve e-mail. At a company level, a policy discouraging the sending of trivial e-mail could save hundreds of hours of time for every employee every year—and eliminate the need to read items that have no value to your function.

Using Intranets and the Internet

Both powerful tools, the Internet and intranets pose some crucial challenges when it comes to formulating an overall communication strategy. Evaluate:

- Security, including encryption of documents via public and private keys and degrees of access
- Cost
    The time required to produce a document
    The distribution barriers and advantages
- Speed
- Color and complexity (for example the use of Visio and Acrobat software solutions)

Document Management Systems

The key to successful use of the Internet and intranets is the use of document management systems ideas. This topic is discussed in detail in Chapter 2.

Putting Paper-Intensive Tasks On-Line

Companies experience greater efficiencies by putting databases, inventory control (JIT, etc.), advertising, marketing, customer service, benefits information, personnel manuals, newsletters, and management announcements/bulletins on an intranet. The sky's the limit. Employees who can use electronic document management systems become better informed and are able to make faster, more qualified decisions.

 DEVELOPING EFFECTIVE BUSINESS COMMUNICATION WITHIN TEAMS

Intranets and the Internet offer parallel advantages for facilitating communication to groups and teams. To optimize communication advantages, teams need to do the following:

- Identify requirements.
- Identify resources/strengths/barriers (for example, the presence/absence of processes, personal skills, interpersonal, hardware, software, and standards).
- Establish/adopt templates/standards.
- Establish/adopt/implement processes (especially a writing and editing process, document sharing, and project management).

DEVELOPING EFFECTIVE BUSINESS COMMUNICATION SKILLS AS AN INDIVIDUAL

For an individual contributor, some choices are constrained by company-level and team or project decisions. However, a decision to improve specific skills can be made by individuals and can be done without extensive support, especially when justified as part of a personal career advancement effort. To optimize communication, individuals need to do the following:

- Identify requirements and define products that meet those requirements.
- Determine resources, strengths, and barriers (hardware, software, processes, personal skills, knowledge, etc.).
- Implement processes.
- Improve personal skills.

INTEGRATED SUPPLY CHAINS AND RESOURCE MANAGEMENT

Over the last several years, the idea of supply-chain linkages in manufacturing environments has gained momentum as the need for more effective sharing of information throughout a company, and with outside vendors and customers, has increased. If a company cannot efficiently share information, it is unlikely that supply-chain linkages can be identified or continuously improved, which can lead to a noncompetitive situation.

Companies need to create processes that enable their employees to appropriately and successfully share information within and across organizational units. Companies that do not develop and encourage the use of such processes give up potential competitive advantages and underutilize the strengths of their employees.

In Figure 1.4, we show a simplified view of potential linkages among groups in a simplified supply chain. An important communication question is: What barriers exist in current processes that inhibit sharing of information? From a management communication perspective, are there opportunities to share and leverage information that can improve processes and products? Are there opportunities to increase communication efficiency and eliminate barriers? Pertinent questions include the following:

- What information can Market Research share with Hardware Design that will help develop a better product?

- What can Customer Service share with Software Design that will improve ease of operation for customers or help hardware designers create a more dependable machine?

- How can Manufacturing and Hardware Design work together to create an easier-to-build machine?

- Can Logistics and Distribution and Customer Service decrease the quantity of low-use spare parts held in multiple locations by Customer Service?

- Do field technicians have information (for example, part reliability) that is not shared with Hardware Design for lack of an appropriate communications mechanism?

- What information does the Corporate Strategy group need—and need to share?

Supply-Chain Linkages in Nonmanufacturing Environments

Supply-chain-like linkage problems are also inherent in service organizations. Nonprofit and government organizations have customers, boards of directors, and customers or clients, and the problems associated with

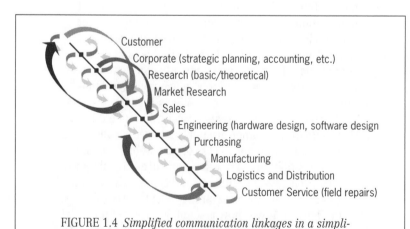

FIGURE 1.4 *Simplified communication linkages in a simplified supply chain (manufacturing).*

effective communication in a business environment
also exist in those organizations. The communication
relationships shown in Figures 1.1 and 1.2 are critical.
The groups shown in Figure 1.4 obviously will vary
depending on the organization, group, or agency.

MANAGEMENT STYLES AND COMMUNICATION STRATEGIES

We advocate using win-win approaches to management, problem solving, and communication because
they increase the efficiency of individuals, teams, areas,
and companies. If these approaches are linked to
appropriate incentive and reward systems (for example, performance pay, merit pay, or profit sharing), they
can lead to performance improvements at all levels of
an organization.

Effecting Change

If your company, area, or team (or yourself as an individual) does not use win-win approaches, how can you
implement a change in your communication styles? We
suggest using the ideas of Fisher and Ury, Deming, and
others to eliminate barriers to effective communication
and increased productivity.

END POINT

From a strategic perspective, improved communication
enhances the performance of the whole company, from
sharing knowledge and innovative ideas to being able to
make faster and better decisions. Deciding to improve
overall communication requires support at a company,
team or group, and individual contributor level.

Win-win approaches can promote successful communication, and change a win-lose to a win-win or
interest-based approach. It is important to stress how
the win-win approach can benefit individuals, teams,
and the entire company.

2

Document Management in an Electronic Age

Over the last several years, a new focus on business communication has emerged: that of computerized document management. Document management is a concern at all levels and for all organizations. This is due in part to the increased use of computer programs to generate and manage documents, as well as the need for increased linkages among business groups and functions. Businesses are also communicating in new ways; whereas previously a group of people would meet to talk about an issue, they now often address issues by conference calls, videoconferencing, and/or e-mail in an effort to decrease meetings, eliminate barriers created by distance, and increase efficiency.

The increasing use of e-mail, databases, spreadsheets, and other forms of communication leads to the creation and retention of more documents. And this increased production, retention, and use of documents creates a need to evaluate work processes, workflow, and documents from the perspective of a document cycle: the origination, filing, use/retrieval, security, retention, and the destruction of documents.

In this section, we will highlight some of the key ideas that are moving to the forefront; however, to gain a fuller understanding of these rapidly evolving issues and potential solutions, we strongly recommend a quick search of the Internet. You will discover tens of thousands of sites, documents, consulting firms, and software providers that focus on document management.

We will briefly review some of the approaches being taken by major corporate players in document management systems: Xerox (DocuShare), IBM (Documentum Enterprise Document Management Systems, EDMS), Microsoft (Microsoft Exchange, BackOffice, and Document Management Extensions), Lotus (Lotus Notes and Domino), and Adobe (Acrobat, Acrobat Reader), among others.

Table 2.1 shows software solutions and web site locations of companies with major document management efforts.

CHANGES IN DOCUMENT MANAGEMENT

As recently as 10 years ago, the use of hard-copy documents was the preferred way of conducting business. That preference is now giving way to the use of electronic documents that are linked in complex electronic systems. Today, the use of e-mail is likely to be deemed a more effective way to share information. Several years ago, a report would be written, and sharing that report would mean copying or printing it and then mailing or otherwise physically delivering it. Today, reports are efficiently shared over intranets and the Internet, and the primary focus is not only on how to get the report printed and distributed, but also on who should be given what levels of electronic access (such as the right to modify content) to these documents. This is a serious issue related to the security of the document.

TABLE 2.1 WEB SITE ADDRESSES FOR DOCUMENT MANAGEMENT SOFTWARE SOLUTIONS

Company	Software Solution	Web Site(s)
Xerox	DocuShare	xerox.com/products/docushare
IBM	EDMS	edms.solutions.ibm.com
Microsoft	Exchange, BackOffice, Extensions	microsoft.com *and* 80-20.com
Adobe	Acrobat, PDF*fusion*	adobe.com *and* docctrl.com/fusion
Lotus	Lotus Notes, Domino	lotus.com/products
Axiom	Cabinet NG	cabinetng.com
Aviator	Aviator for Lotus Notes	aviatorsoftware.com

KEY CONCEPT

DOCUMENT LIFE CYCLES

Software solutions are driving changes in how companies view the management of documents and document life cycles. Document life cycle issues include the following:

- Origination
- Filing/use/retrieval
- Security
- Retention/destruction

Origination

When evaluating strategies for the creation of documents, a companywide perspective should include:

- Project requirements
- Sufficiency and compatibility of software programs and data
- Training that users will need to perform required functions
- Technical (computer) support needed
- Total cost of ownership issues

Any one of these issues can be an extremely expensive barrier to eliminate after a software decision has been made.

Project Requirements

The capabilities of document management systems are extensive, and in-depth evaluation is required to determine which system to implement. Top-down management of this decision would be counterproductive. Input is needed from multiple layers of management (including project managers) and also from your technological staff. The people who hold critical knowledge about the requirements for document management and the barriers that need to be overcome are not high-level managers, but rather, those doing day-to-day document-handling tasks, be they database managers, assistants, or employees in contact with external clients and vendors. A document management system's value extends beyond the immediate internal needs of a company; additional value comes from your improved ability to exchange data with sources external to the company (vendors, bidders, customers, etc.).

Sufficiency and Compatibility

Many heavily promoted document management systems and tools, such as Xerox's DocuShare, IBM's EDMS, and Adobe's Acrobat, are designed to support multiple software packages and operating platforms.

An evaluation of a document management system or tool should include its ability to handle your current software and documents, files from your legacy applications, scanned documents, and data from external sources (again, vendors, bidders, customers).

Another valuable by-product of document management systems is the ability to implement document templates that will produce consistency and eliminate the need to reinvent reports or other document formats/templates for every project. Reports will be easier to write and you'll be able to connect them to other reports in your database.

Training

Training employees to use document management systems is costly; but *not* training them is often more costly.

Technical (Computer) Support

One of the major requirements for effective document management is excellent technical (computer hardware, software, and networking) support. You can find a wealth of information on document management support through vendors' web sites, such as Xerox and IBM.

Filing/Use/Retrieval

The filing, use, and/or retrieval of documents are critical issues. For those of us who use every available flat surface to accumulate paperwork, using file drawers is overwhelming, and storing electronic (nonvisible) documents can be catastrophic. Equally true, anyone who has worked on a multiyear project or who is part of a major corporation that is continually growing or downsizing knows that well-organized document classification, sorting, and retrieval systems are essential.

Linking and Locating Documents

When a company has multiple projects running concurrently, or thousands of pages of documentation (and revisions and updates) on one project, being able to locate a document quickly is critical. Being able to cross-reference documents (be it by project, employee, raw material, or another basis) is also a must.

Creating Documents on Demand

Document management systems can improve the production and distribution of customized "documents on demand." Producing documents on demand eliminates the need to print and store multiple (in some cases thousands) of copies of manuals and other documentation, which can greatly reduce waste (especially in terms of revisions and updates). To remain competitive, companies need to develop document classification, filing, and retrieval strategies that not only handle existing requirements, but also have the flexibility to grow as requirements change and expand. Adobe Acrobat, a viable solution for sharing documents, is growing in acceptance. (See Table 2.2.)

Security

Generating electronic documents has created new security problems. For example, in a recent case, an employee of a major East Coast–based corporation, fearing upcoming layoffs, e-mailed years of her confidential research work to her sister at another corporation based on the West Coast. It is quite possible for an employee to either copy, alter, relocate, or destroy years of work in a matter of seconds if the proper backup and access rights to files have not been established or maintained. Document management systems allow different levels of access (i.e., none, read-only, write) to be assigned to different users, which can help mitigate such problems.

Retention and/or Destruction

The retention and/or destruction of documents has gained visibility in recent years, in part due to high-profile lawsuits (tobacco, asbestos, silicon breast

TABLE 2.2 TECH TOOLS: ADOBE ACROBAT, A VIABLE SOLUTION FOR CREATING SECURE, INDEXABLE DOCUMENTS

Adobe Acrobat, a viable solution for sharing documents, is growing in acceptance. Acrobat's Portable Document Format (PDF) files allow for the electronic distribution of most documents across multiple platforms and using any media. Using Acrobat, documents (including legacy documents) can be fully indexed and searched on-line. Acrobat can also significantly reduce electronic file sizes by identifying and eliminating the storage of redundant objects and information within files. In addition, those files can be locked to ensure that they are distributed only with the content you created.

For more information on the latest version of Adobe Acrobat and Adobe Reader (currently a free-of-charge program for reading Adobe Acrobat files), visit the Internet:

http//:www.adobe.com

implants, etc.) where millions of pages of documentation have been subpoenaed.

As a result, more companies are establishing policies regarding if and when specific documents should be retained or destroyed. (And no, you can't wait to make that decision until after you've received a subpoena; destroying documents at that point will probably be a felony in the United States.) Equally important, some documents—for example, inventions, patents, and corporate policies—need careful evaluation before they are destroyed.

END POINT

Using a document management system and establishing a coordinated document life cycle policy can increase productivity and decrease liability-related issues. Companies need to establish clear and consistent document management systems that involve individuals at all levels of the organization in order to ensure their effective implementation and maintenance.

Business Writing and Editing

It would be rare to find an executive who doesn't count business writing as one of the most important and significant parts of his or her job description. Most executives and managers spend a significant portion of the workday generating e-mail, memos, and letters. They also frequently write reports, proposals, and requests for proposals. Yet many executives have very little formal training in how to write beyond the freshman composition courses required in college. The business writer has two main concerns:

- How can I write more effectively and efficiently?
- How can I get the results, the response, I want to get?

In Part 2, we address these concerns by advocating a systematic writing and editing process. Using a writing and editing process will (1) help you make better decisions about your writing and (2) help you identify and avoid common writing problems.

A writing and editing process is useful and cost-effective; it saves time and improves results by helping *both* the writers and the readers of a document. As a writer, you will learn to organize documents so that their logic and structure are visually clear to your readers, thus helping your readers to quickly grasp your key points. If you have the right content, you'll get the results you want.

Part 2 (Chapters 3 through 10) contains information designed to help you improve your writing skills. Chapters 3, 4, and 5 present ideas that are directly linked to the writing and editing process. Chapters 6 through 10 provide specific information on how to improve specific types of documents. Topics include the following:

- Using writing and editing processes
- Developing the logic and structure of your documents
- Organizing the layout and design of your documents
- Preparing different types of documents
  - E-mail
  - Memos
  - Business letters
  - Reports and executive summaries
  - Proposals and requests for proposals

Our goal in this cluster of chapters is to create linkages to the writing and editing process, to provide useful tips on avoiding common problems, and to help you create high-quality documents that require significantly less effort and time to prepare and use!

If you get in the habit of using a systematic writing and editing process, we guarantee that you'll write more persuasively and effectively—and save time and money!

Using Writing and Editing Processes

If you are like most managers and executives, you're spending too much time writing reports, proposals, memos, e-mail, and letters. In this section, we demonstrate our "writing and editing process," which can help you decide whether writing is the most appropriate way to get your message across and, if so, how to write more efficiently and effectively.

Using a specific writing and editing process will help you systematically organize your goals, evaluate your logic, build stronger arguments, and avoid common errors.

The four primary steps to the writing and editing process are *prewriting, drafting, editing,* and *postwriting* (see Figure 3.1).

However, you will find that your writing will be easier and more effective if you use our six-step writing and editing process (see Figure 3.2). This six-step process uses three sequential editing steps to save editing time and generate more effective documents.

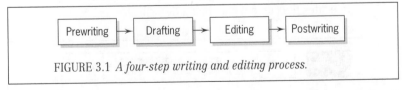

FIGURE 3.1 *A four-step writing and editing process.*

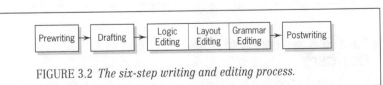

FIGURE 3.2 *The six-step writing and editing process.*

MAKE THE PROCESS A HABIT

Think of the writing and editing process as a set of good habits, not as a laborious task. When you use a writing and editing process, you're replacing inefficient, unconscious writing habits with a systematic process that will improve your message's effectiveness.

Most of us share at least one inefficient writing habit: We try to perform several editing tasks simultaneously. For example, we try to check a 50-page document for errors in verb tenses while simultaneously deciding where to insert figures or tables to reduce text and worrying about including content needed by a senior manager. Then, about 35 pages into the report, we notice a major error, become distracted, and go back to the beginning to try and correct it. We then find another problem, and pretty soon, we forget what we have and have not checked. All this rechecking and reediting becomes very time-consuming, which is why a systematic process can save you time and effort.

CLARIFY YOUR GOALS

Many business writers revise and revise and revise their documents because they don't know what they really want to accomplish. They don't have clearly defined goals. By using our writing and editing process, you will be able to do the following:

- Define your message.
- Identify and meet the requirements of those using your materials.
- Work more efficiently by improving the organization of your work processes and materials.
- Evaluate your logic, build stronger and clearer arguments, and avoid common errors.

In this chapter, we define and explain our process steps. In subsequent chapters, we demonstrate how to apply these steps to a variety of documents. We will guide you through our writing and editing process with a series of figures that illustrate the process and show you where you are in the process. A shadowed box indicates the current step being described.

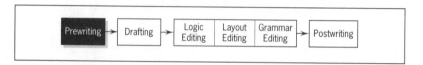

KEY CONCEPT

PREWRITING

Prewriting, the first step in the writing and editing process, is a decision-making step that helps you:

- Decide if your document is appropriate to write.
- Determine what to include.
- Avoid common initial writing errors.
- Avoid writer's block.

Many people writing in business settings get off on the wrong foot because they start to write without knowing where they want to end up. Having only a general idea of what you want to say means you're not quite ready to begin writing. As a result, you'll probably have to revise what you've written because you haven't evaluated the following items:

- Where are you trying to go? What's your objective, purpose, or goal?
- Who will be reading the material? Who is your audience?
- What do your readers already know?
- What do your readers need to know to evaluate your points?
- What action do you want readers to take?

The prewriting process includes answering these and related questions. Table 3.1 provides you with specific questions that will help you make some strategic decisions about what your document needs to say. Additional information on defining your purpose and analyzing your audience can be found in Chapters 11 and 12.

Prewriting Helps You Avoid Writer's Block

At the start of writing seminars and classes, we always ask, "How many of you get writer's block when you are writing memos or business letters or reports?" Typically, over 40 percent indicate that writer's block is a problem.

However, when you make decisions about your goals and content at the prewriting stage, you effectively eliminate any doubts about what you need to write. Your task becomes one of systematically organizing and writing down your key points, drafting your material, editing it, and then evaluating it.

Remember, too, that deciding *not* to write or deciding *not* to include some information in a written document or public presentation can be a viable alternative. Although we provide instruction on how to write, we advocate writing only when you've decided that it is necessary. Table 3.2 presents some key issues to consider in deciding whether you need to write.[1,2]

In summary, remember the following key points about prewriting:

TABLE 3.1 PREWRITING QUESTIONS

Using the following questions during your prewriting process can help you make key decisions about the direction the document takes.

"What do I want to accomplish?"

- What are my primary objectives?
- What do I want my readers to do or *not* do, and by when?
- How important is my reader's action or inaction?
- How much effort and cost are justified—in reading or in writing?

"Who is going to read the document?"

- Who are my intended readers?
- Who are other potential readers—now and in the future?

"What content, ideas, or data are needed in the document?"

- What do my readers already know?
- What do my readers want to know?
- What specific content, ideas, and/or data do I include or exclude?
- What format (memo, letter, report, phone) do I use to distribute the information?

"How can I best organize my points into a coherent argument?"

- What organizational plan (e.g., problem-solution) will link my ideas/data?
- Should I use several organizational plans (e.g., time sequences, geographic locations, problem/solutions) to organize ideas within and across sections?
- Can I improve my transitions and improve the strength of my argument?

"Do my layout and design make this document clear?"

- Are my design elements (heads, subheads, bullets, margins, bolding, fonts, graphics, etc.) making my logic and structure both logically and visually clear?
- Am I using design elements consistently, thus reducing the need for revisions—especially for group projects?
- Am I using figures, tables, charts, and/or graphics to advance my arguments and reduce text?

- Prewriting is a decision-making step.
- Prewriting leads to success because it makes you think before you start writing.
- Thinking before writing and knowing your goal eliminates rewriting and wasted effort.
- Prewriting helps you determine the type of document you need to create (persuasive or informative,

TABLE 3.2 WHY WRITE?

Why do we write at all? Most often it's because written records:

- Encourage precise thought and control of language.
- Can reduce misunderstandings and ensure uniform instructions.
- Can overcome problems of distance and time.
- Facilitate retention of information.
- Allow readers to read and reread on their own schedules.
- Allow controlled, consistent, and rapid distribution.
- Fix responsibility (e.g., for authorship or actions).
- Provide a record and can be checked for accuracy.

However, poorly written documents can undermine your goals. Keep the following in mind:

- Ineffective, unclear, or ill-conceived documents create confusion.
- Documents are costly to create and to read. (How much do you earn an hour? How much do your readers earn an hour? How restricted or strategically valuable is their time?)
- The amount of time it takes to create a document can lead to critical delays and impersonal, one-way communication.

In *Business Reports: Oral and Written*,[2] Ruch and Crawford (1988) indicate memos, letters, and reports are useful for documenting a process or creating a legal record. This suggests that you:

- Don't write if you don't want to create legal records.
- Write (or elicit) a letter/memo to help create legal records.

To create more effective documents, know your audience. Know what they need. Know what you want done or what you want to say or accomplish, and state it clearly. Most important, if you can't write coherently, get a second opinion on your document. A poorly written document can become a permanent record of your error and a source of problems that are more complex than the ones you are trying to solve.

long or short, etc.) to fulfill your goals and your readers' needs.

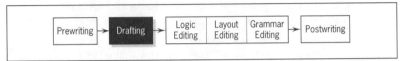

| Prewriting → | **Drafting** → | Logic Editing | Layout Editing | Grammar Editing | → Postwriting |

KEY CONCEPT

DRAFTING

Creating a draft version of a document—a version that you intend to modify to improve its organization, logic, structure, persuasiveness, and/or grammar—is a common practice, especially with important reports, proposals, and business letters.

Drafting is a straightforward step if you have completed the prewriting process.

What points should you consider when you start to draft a document? First, review the four basic questions associated with the prewriting step:

- What do you want the document to accomplish?
- Who is going to read the document?
- How can you effectively organize or link your points into a coherent argument?
- What layout and design standards will make it a successful (professional) document?

After you've answered these questions, your drafting process steps are as follows:

- Complete any needed research or data gathering.
- Expand your notes and identify your key points.
- Double-check your notes for other key points.
- Choose an organizational plan or plans to link your ideas, such as moving from problem to solution or writing chronologically.
- Improve the impact of your writing:

  Use your readers' viewpoints and address their concerns.

  State your key point, action, or requirement in your first paragraph.

Key Differences between Editing and Drafting

When you're drafting, your goal is to get your ideas down, not to have the document letter-perfect. You shouldn't stop every five words to validate the logic of your argument, to modify a head or subhead, to review your phrasing, or to correct your spelling. Those are editing steps, not drafting steps. If something seems problematic while you are drafting your material, just highlight it, type a couple of stars beside it, leave an underscored blank (_____) after it, circle it, or underline it, but don't stop and try to fix it. If you stop, you will interrupt the flow of your basic ideas and linkages. If you draft and edit simultaneously, you will tend to get into endless loops and revisions.

Don't stop to create or insert figures, tables, or graphics during drafting. That, too, is part of the editing process. Just note where you'll need to add a figure or table. Your goal is to keep ideas flowing and to focus on your purpose. Fix and tighten the linkages among your ideas when you edit.

Don't stop to edit your grammar and spelling. That is not a drafting step. In fact, fixing your grammar is your third editing step.

During your first editing step, when you edit for logic (your conceptual or content points), you will probably eliminate material from your draft, so getting it letter-perfect while you are drafting wastes time and breaks your thought patterns, which can lead to multiple loops and revisions. It is important that you allocate time to edit your work.

How rare is it to find people who don't need to edit their work? *Very.* We have met only two or three people who can perhaps bypass this step, and we don't include ourselves among them!

 Treat all of your documents as drafts, even electronic messages. Set your e-mail messages aside for a few minutes before clicking the Send button. When you come back and look at them, you will often have a new perspective, and you might see glaring errors as well as ways to make the message more effective. Best of all, you might save yourself and your department or company some embarrassment.

 If you use a word processing program, such as Microsoft Word, that has automatic spell checking and grammar checking, consider turning off those features. Many people find it hard to ignore those red and green squiggly lines, but seeing what they've misspelled or misphrased can break their concentration. Some writers find it more helpful to complete a grammar and spell check after having drafted the material.

EDITING

Editing is the *key* to creating a good document. Many writing processes use steps that are parallel to our prewriting, drafting, editing, and postwriting steps.[1] However, we break the editing step into *three sequential substeps,* which helps you work more efficiently. Our three-step editing process allows you to improve your draft document systematically without wasting time and effort.

Step 1: Editing the Logic and Structure

Editing logic and structure to enhance the flow of information is the first editing substep. Unfortunately, it is also the most frequently ignored. When business writers assume that all they have to do is start writing without choosing an organizational plan, they end up with documents that ramble.

One way to provide structure and logical organizational patterns, especially with longer documents, is to use the popular "Army approach" to teaching, speaking, and writing:

1. Tell your readers what you're going to tell them.

2. Tell it to them.

3. Tell them what you've told them.

Here's a parallel approach in writing:

1. Use an introduction—either a sentence, a full introduction, a table of contents, or an executive summary.

2. Make your points concisely, and use heads, subheads, and graphics to emphasize them.

3. Summarize and conclude.

You can also improve the logic, structure and organization of your documents by asking yourself the following key questions:

- Can your reader immediately identify you, your position, and your company?

- Is the action you want the reader to take clear in your first or last paragraph?

- Is the action you are going to take clear in your first or last paragraph?

- Are your recommendations clear, supported, and in your first or last paragraph?

- Are your organizational plan and content easy to understand?

- Would a different organizational plan make your content easier to understand?

- Can readers skim the document (does it have good heads, subheads, transitions, etc.)?

- Are your assumptions justified and supported?

- Is the content factual, correct, and persuasive?

Step 2: Editing Layout and Design

Good layout and design make the logic of your message visually clear.

One important, yet often overlooked, task is to determine where you need to add graphics, figures, and/or tables to make your message easier to follow or to strengthen your argument. Include a transition that helps the reader see how to use it, and create a transition that moves your reader to your next point.

Don't just plunk a graphic, figure, or table into your text and assume that it is self-explanatory or that it automatically leads to your next idea. A figure or a table on a page of text material is a magnet for a reader's eye. It is one of the first things a person will scan. If it is well done, it will help drive home your key point on that page or in that section. Make sure you label it clearly and refer to it in the text of the document.

How do you choose your layout and design elements? Most of us just highlight, bold, and/or add italics at will. There are better ways. You need to take your reader's perspective and evaluate how you would react if you received this document. Table 3.3 provides some questions to ask yourself as you evaluate your document for organization, layout, design, and style sheets.

Use a style sheet. Style sheets allow you to establish and use consistent formats for paragraphs, heads, subheads, fonts, italic, bold, and so forth. If you establish your layout and design criteria before you start, you'll save yourself and your team extensive time and revision. Word processing packages with style sheets are now quite common (unfortunately, however, some are poorly designed). Take the time to learn how to use a style sheet effectively, especially if your company prefers a particular style.

Step 3: Editing for Grammar

The third editing substep is editing your grammar. This process is often the only editing step that many writers complete. It includes such things as identifying and fix-

TABLE 3.3 ORGANIZATION, LAYOUT, AND DESIGN

Look at your finished document in terms of layout and design:

- If I received this document, would I read it or toss it aside for later?
- Would I be more likely to read the document if key points and organization were easier to see visually?
- Can I make the linkages among ideas visually clearer by changing heads and subheads or using figures or tables?
- Is the document visually pleasing? Is it in an appropriate business format? Did I use clear laser typeface(s) or font(s)? Does it fit together as whole (font, margins, heads, etc.)?
- Would adding color emphasize my key points better or be a distraction?
- Does my document look like others my company creates?

ing commas and other punctuation problems, poor phrasing, subject-verb agreement problems, misused pronouns, and article errors. But editing for grammar only does not address the equally important components of your document's logic and structure, layout and design.

Often, writers correct grammar errors at the wrong time—before they're finished with the editing process. This wastes time, and you run the risk of forgetting to edit for grammar after making last-minute fixes to the logic or content.

Check for grammar errors by reading aloud. To help identify grammar errors in a document, treat it as you would one of your favorite children's books. If you can read your document aloud without pausing or stumbling, it's probably well written. If you stumble over a sentence that you yourself wrote, what will your readers do?

Be cautious when using grammar checkers. It is helpful is to run a grammar checker, but don't expect perfection. Every generation of grammar checkers is greatly improved, but many grammar checkers are only about 40 percent accurate. They identify both false positives and false negatives; you have to know enough grammar to recognize when they are wrong. If you are like most of us, you have not taken a grammar test since ninth grade, so consider completing the self-diagnostic test for grammar in Appendix A of this book. It can help you identify and correct your personal error patterns.

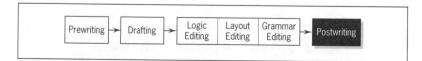

POSTWRITING

KEY CONCEPT Many writing and editing processes end with the editing step. However, editing is *not* the end of the process. When you're done, set your memo or report aside for a few hours and then check it again for problematic errors before you send it out. And before you send it, check with your manager or supervisor to be sure anything you've promised can be delivered. If you don't regularly complete these two simple steps, we guarantee you will eventually regret it, especially if you cannot provide the service or product.

In the postwriting process, change your perspective from writer to reader. Among the postwriting questions you should ask yourself are the following:

- Have I met the reader's requirements or does she need more information?
- Am I writing statements that I'll later regret?
- Did I proofread my document? Should a colleague proof it? Is it worth proofreading twice?
- Did I spell check and grammar check?
- Have I arranged for reproduction, distribution, and storage?
- Do I need clearance to send or distribute the document?
- If I was angry when I wrote it, have I let it sit overnight?

END POINT

The sequential, multiple-step writing and editing process is effective because it helps writers segment what appears to be an overwhelmingly complex task into a series of manageable steps. Using a writing and editing process can help you accomplish the following:

- Build documents that are complete, supported, persuasive, and effective.
- Save yourself and your readers time and money.
- Spend your weekends with your family, playing golf or bringing balance to your life!

CHAPTER 4

Developing the Logic and Structure of Documents

In the writing and editing process presented in Chapter 3, we noted that creating an effective, well-organized, written document requires the writer to address three broad topics in sequence:

- Logic and structure
- Layout and design
- Grammar

The most easily recognized errors in documents are often those associated with grammar, including spelling errors and inconsistencies in phrasing. These errors are becoming more easily identified, if not corrected, by the use of word processing programs that include spelling- and grammar-checking programs, which, although not optimal, can serve as a helpful way to double-check your own proofreading and editing.

But, obviously, no software program can adequately tell you how to better organize your logic and structure, or your design layout. In fact, structure problems are often exacerbated by errors in layout and design. For example, if the logic and structure of a document is faulty, the visual cues, the layout and design of the document, cannot be effective and may, in fact, misdirect the readers' attention. Together, these two categories of problems are important causes of unpersuasive documents.

In this chapter, we address issues related to improving the logic and structure of your documents.

- Think first.
- Create an organizational plan.

- Build strong arguments.
- Use figures and tables.

THINK FIRST

Before you start writing, you need to *think*. Seriously. It is extremely important to spend a couple of minutes just thinking about your purpose and your readers. We suggest some questions you may wish to ask yourself in the prewriting phase of the writing and editing process in Chapter 3. Additional considerations are addressed in Chapter 12, "Analyzing your Audience." The same basic principles apply to both writing and presenting orally.

To improve the logic and structure of a document, consider the following:

- Identify who will be reading your document.
- Decide what you want your audience to do after reading your material.
- Identify what they want to know, their needs or requirements, what they already know, and what they don't know.
- Decide if your goal is to persuade or to give an informative overview of ideas.
- Identify the key points that you need to address.
- Determine how to order or sequence those points most effectively.
- Choose an organizational plan (for example, give the problem and a proposed solution, the costs and the benefits, and an implementation plan).
- Use sufficient material to support your points.
- Help your reader see at a glance how your ideas fit together.

If you spend some time thinking about these issues before you begin writing, you will find it easier to organize your ideas and structure your document.

CREATE AN ORGANIZATIONAL PLAN

Good organization in effective communication cannot be overstated. Good organization helps your readers to better understand your message and improves your credibility. Novice writers sometimes use an organizational plan we have dubbed "the random generation of nonconnected ideas." This is definitely not an effective way to present information or to enhance its retention. Rather, effective writers use commonly identified and standard organizational patterns. Effective summaries of organizational plans have been developed by Penrose, Rasberry, and Myers in *Advanced Business Communication*[1]*;* in Sterkel's *Effective Business and Professional Letters*[2]*;* and others.

Penrose, Rasberry, and Myers stress that you can enhance the retention of information by using an appropriate organizational pattern, such as:

- Chronology
- Causal
- Structure/function
- Order of importance
- Problem-solution
- Spatial/geography
- Topical

These plans are basically self-explanatory. For example, *chronology* implies that you link ideas by order of time—for example, what is to be done in the first, second, third, and fourth fiscal quarters. These plans are extremely useful because they provide options that can help you establish a framework for emphasizing different types of information and relationships.

 A common mistake is to believe that you can use only one organizational plan or one logical structure in a document. Often, more than one can work, and your task is to anticipate which plan will work most effectively with your readers. In many instances, it is helpful to use several organizational plans in a document to show different interrelationships among ideas. For example, an overall organizational plan for a memo might be to discuss a problem and a solution to that problem. The solution to that problem, however, might need its own organizational plan—for example, a plan emphasizing the quarterly implementation (chronology) of the proposed solution and/or the costs and benefits associated with specific aspects of the solution.

Direct and Indirect Organizational Plans

Karen Sterkel, among others, suggests that it is helpful to establish a direct or indirect psychological plan. For example, you can construct effective routine memos, letters, and reports by using a *direct plan,* a plan that presents a concise main idea in the first sentence or paragraph to focus the reader. Next, you present your main ideas, add supporting details, and add a close.

In contrast, an *indirect plan* can be effectively used for bad news or unfavorable memos, letters, or reports. In an indirect plan, Sterkel suggests placing your main idea in middle of your material. First, you develop and present your supporting ideas to act as a buffer. You state your reasons for a decision, offer a compromise, and close. Sterkel suggests that the indirect plan is effective for persuasive documents because you get the readers' attention, give details, minimize obstacles, anticipate action, and close.

BUILD STRONG ARGUMENTS

In addition to the use of organizational plans, we suggest building stronger arguments in your documents and presentations by eliminating two common logic and structure problems:

- Unsupported statements
- The so-what problem

Unsupported Statements

We often see inexperienced managers who fall into the trap of making unsupported statements: They state their ideas as facts; they fail to support their points with data; they use invalid data; and/or they fail to use appropriate statistical analyses of data. As a result, readers are left floundering on their own to develop the missing data or analyses. Often, writers fail to supply the data to prove their point or to properly analyze it because they were not thinking clearly or had not properly evaluated the logic of their arguments.

Remember, facts must be supported by verifiable information. Citing highly credible sources in your document strengthens your image and avoids any suggestion of plagiarism.

The So-What Problem

Larry Matteson, retired vice president at Eastman Kodak, while teaching at the Simon Graduate School of Business at the University of Rochester, often emphasized the "so-what" problem to MBA candidates. As writers and as managers, we often fail to make connections among our ideas for our readers. We assume they know where we are going. We assume they know how to get there. We even assume they agree we should go there! All these assumptions are faulty, and they prevent us from building organized arguments that help our readers see not only our end points, but also the processes and data that helped us get there. In addition, we fail to tell them the *reasons* we should get there—the so-what!

Avoid the so-what problem. Make your statements, give your assumptions and supporting data, and eliminate extraneous information. Close the loop and make certain that your reader understands your point, your conclusion, the value you are trying to point out. Make certain your readers get to the end of your memos, reports, or proposals without a lingering, "So what?"

◆K◆E◆Y◆ USE FIGURES AND TABLES
CONCEPT

One of the most effective ways to help your readers grasp and follow the logic and structure of your materials is to help them visualize your ideas. Graphics, tables, figures, and graphs help accomplish this in at least three ways.

First, properly designed graphics explain complex information in ways that highlight the relationships among ideas, thus providing insights into those relationships. Rather than writing two or three paragraphs of text to provide a conceptual overview of the material, it is often possible to show complex relationships visually.

Second, graphics, tables, and figures force a writer to analyze and better understand, from a reader's perspective, the ideas that are being presented. Tables and figures do not lend themselves to rambling.

Third, graphs, figures, and tables simplify and emphasize key points. Figures, tables, charts, and graphs catch a reader's eye and help to isolate your key points. By focusing a reader's attention in this way and by visually displaying the connections between your ideas, your argument becomes easier to follow.

Designing an Effective Table or Figure

Creating an effective table or figure involves an analysis process, a design process, and consistency.

Analysis

First, you need to decide what you want to accomplish. This is the audience analysis task that comes with the prewriting questions and the audience analysis for presentations (see pages 24–27 and 109–117).

Design

Second, you need to decide how to emphasize your key point or simplify the complexity of the information. For example, Figure 4.1 shows how you can simplify a complex set of information by eliminating implicit information (the zeros that function as placeholders, in this example). Further, you can add highlighting (by changing color or fonts or by adding italics or bolding) so that readers see at a glance the key points in a complex figure.

In addition, use an effective label or title, one that calls attention to the point you want to emphasize. The

Before

Part	SF1	SF2	Sea	Dal	Atl	Bos	Tor
1AB1	0	0	10	20	15	0	0
1AB2	0	0	10	20	15	0	0
2BC1	25	0	0	0	0	25	25
2BC2	25	0	0	0	0	25	25
2BC3	5	0	0	0	0	5	5
3CD1	0	50	0	0	0	0	0
3CD2	0	50	0	0	0	50	0
3CD3	0	50	0	0	0	50	0
3CD4	0	50	0	0	0	50	0

Location

After

Inventory Stock and Shortages by Warehouse Location/City

Shaded cells indicate critical shortages on 10/31/2002

Warehouse Location/City→

Part ↓	SF1	SF2	Sea	Dal	Atl	Bos	Tor
1AB1			10	20	15		
1AB2			10	20	15		
2BC1	25					25	25
2BC2	25					25	25
2BC3	5					5	5
3CD1		50					
3CD2		50				50	
3CD3		50				50	
3CD4		50				50	

FIGURE 4.1 *Improve tables and figures by eliminating implicit information, adding highlighting, and using effective labels and titles to focus readers.*

title of a figure, graph, or table can serve the same function as a subject line in a memo or an e-mail: It focuses the reader.

Consistency

Consistency among multiple graphs, tables, and figures is another key factor in a document and in presentations that are linked to written documents. Help your readers by focusing on your information; don't force them to spend time trying to decode variations in your visual cues and emphases. For example, if you use a 5 percent gray background to highlight a key cell in a table or spreadsheet, don't switch to bold and eliminate the 5 percent gray background in the next figure, table, or spreadsheet in the same document. If the basic table or figure works for the written portion of your material, don't totally redesign it for your oral presentation. Yes, it might help to add color, but don't switch the rows and the columns without an extremely good reason.

DESIGNING CHARTS, FIGURES, AND TABLES

To be effective, figures and tables don't have to be outsourced to a graphic designer. Frequently, you can use a template from your presentation package to import figures and tables to your written document. Alternatively, you might choose to design a figure or table in your word processor and then import it into your presentation package. Microsoft's Word, Excel, and Power-Point packages all offer user-friendly ways to design charts, tables, and figures that can easily be imported and exported into the other programs for documents and presentations.

When using figures and tables, do more than just stick them into a document; add transitions to help a reader understand:

- Why the figure or table is there
- How to use it
- What it emphasizes
- Where to focus attention

Transitions help the reader move to the next point in your message. Tables and figures should not be added *just* to create white space, to break up the text, or to decorate a page. Tables, figures, and graphs should advance and clarify the logic of your argument.

END POINT

The ways in which you enhance the logic and structure of materials is, in most instances, basic common sense. Unfortunately, we frequently don't take the time to build logic and structure into a document or to verify that they work in the draft material that we have created. Evaluate the logic and structure of all documents, verifying that you have used an appropriate organizational plan, that you have used graphs, figures, and tables to advance your arguments, and that you've knitted your argument together with transitions. Table 4.1 is a checklist to help you improve logic and structure.

It is easy to improve the logic and structure of a document when you adopt the mind-set of your readers. Improve the logic and structure of your documents by

TABLE 4.1 CHECKLIST FOR IMPROVING THE LOGIC AND STRUCTURE OF DOCUMENTS

- ☑ Present a clear focus/purpose/action in first sentence or paragraph.
- ☑ Use statements or visuals that indicate what is coming.
- ☑ Use clear organizational plan(s).
- ☑ Present evenhanded arguments as appropriate.
- ☑ Use logically consistent reasoning.
- ☑ Include supporting detail and/or data with appropriate analyses.
- ☑ Use citations and/or footnotes to document points.
- ☑ Use figures, tables, and graphs to simplify or clarify complex information.
- ☑ Use transitions that link paragraphs and sections.
- ☑ Use the last sentence and/or paragraph to summarize material.

thinking the process through before you start, by implementing organizational plans, by building stronger arguments, and by using figures and tables appropriately. Using these steps can help you create a logical, well-structured document that advances an argument successfully.

Document Layout and Design: Making Your Logic Visually Clear

To the novice writer, the appearance or layout of a document may not seem all that important. As long as the document is neat and has no glaring typographical errors, the writer may assume it's acceptable. However, the layout and design of a document are really crucial for two main reasons:

- Good layout and design of your document can help clarify your logic and structure, which become visible at a glance, allowing the reader to better understand your organization and follow your points.

- Good layout and design concepts also improve crucial esthetic elements of a document. Our seminar and workshop participants almost unanimously indicate that they pay more attention to documents that look professional. Such documents are much better received and are more likely to get the results you need.

At what point do you start to work on the layout and design of your documents? The shaded areas in Figure 5.1 show the steps in which layout and design are considerations. Because these concerns are central to the complete writing and editing process, you need to start thinking about them early on.

FIGURE 5.1 *Layout and design concepts are used during most writing and editing steps.*

As we discuss in Part 4, it is important to establish minimum standards for common layout and design features, especially for team projects (Chapter 20). Individuals also need to establish standards for the various types of documents (memos, e-mail, business or form letters, proposals, reports, etc.) that they commonly create. In the following paragraphs, we discuss which layout and design points you can establish, and often need to revisit, during different writing and editing steps. Figure 5.2 summarizes these points.

 LAYOUT AND DESIGN DURING THE PREWRITING STEP

The prewriting step is the first place where you're concerned with layout and design, because your goal is to save your reader time and to make it easy for him or her to understand your key points. You should be designing the layout of a document to highlight your key points and provide a visual overview of your organization. Evaluating potential layout and design features at this point in the process will also help you recognize when the conceptual organization of your document needs improvement.

Templates and Style Sheets

An effective way to bring consistency to documents and to save design efforts is to use templates and style

---

☑ Use appropriate levels of heads and subheads to show relationships among ideas.

☑ Use displayed lists or bulleted lists to highlight key points and clusters of related points.

☑ Include integrated tables, figures, charts, and graphs that simplify information and ideas.

☑ Vary margins and indentations to show relationships among ideas.

☑ Use sufficient font(s) or typeface(s) and vary the size to add emphasis without adding visual clutter.

☑ Use bolding, italics, and underlining to add visual emphasis.

☑ Use borders, boxes, and shading to show relationships.

☑ Use color to highlight key points.

☑ Use headers or footers to identify document, author/contacts, dates, and pages.

☑ Use white space to reduce concentrated text.

FIGURE 5.2 *Checklist for improving the layout and design of documents.*

sheets. Major companies, such as Xerox, have developed publications manuals designed to help establish corporate visual standards, provide uniform ways to emphasize key points, and save time. Other companies, including Procter & Gamble, traditionally have trained new managers on the "corporate look" for specific types of documents.

The advantages of style sheets or document templates are at least twofold:

- Employees don't have to reinvent the wheel or waste time designing every memo, report, and proposal. This saves extensive amounts of time and money.

- Managers and others who share documents across functional areas or with outside companies become familiar with a generic template and know exactly where to locate key points or sections without searching. This, too, saves extensive amounts of time and money.

USING STYLE SHEETS FROM WORD PROCESSING AND PRESENTATION PROGRAMS

Most small companies don't have the resources to develop extensive standards; however, the style sheets included with first-tier word processing and presentations programs provide very useful options. Such style sheets facilitate the consistent use of styles (for fonts, margins, heads, subheads, and other features such as shading, borders, and color). Software style sheets allow you to design a consistent look within and among documents—designs that might be as simple and effective as using bullets to show action items and due dates in a two-paragraph memo or as complex as formatting a series of proposals to a government agency. Style sheets also allow you to coordinate documents with presentation visuals and materials.

Style Manuals

Another important tool in layout and design is the use of style manuals. Widely used style manuals include the following:

- *The Chicago Manual of Style*[1]
- *Prentice-Hall's Words into Print*[2]
- *The APA Publication Manual* (American Psychological Association)[3]
- *The New York Times Manual of Style and Usage*[4]
- *The Gregg Reference Manual*[5]

These style manuals offer insights into design features and usage information (grammar, reference). For example, when do you hyphenate specific words? How do you use specific honorary titles with international clients? How do you cite a book or a journal article in a report? How do you handle references in footnotes and reference lists? How do you create clear tables and figures? How do you emphasize key points of information?

Consider choosing a single, well-accepted style manual as a universal reference for your company or team. Such a manual will provide a standard source of information that will decrease work interruptions, improve document consistency across the company, facilitate creating a unified document from the work of multiple authors, and help decrease the need for constant reediting.

The design that you develop or choose in your prewriting step should visually emphasize your organizational plan (for example, problem-solution, cause-effect, implementation across fiscal quarters) and effectively demonstrate your points.

LAYOUT AND DESIGN DURING THE DRAFTING AND EDITING STEPS

After establishing layout and design points during your prewriting step, your next writing and editing step is to draft and then edit your materials. When you are editing for content, ask yourself: "Does my logic support my points?" At the same time, try to figure out if your layout and design choices make the information clear. For example, if you have five key points, do those points stand out at first glance, catch the reader's eye, and help provide cues for what you're trying to accomplish?

LAYOUT AND DESIGN DURING THE POSTWRITING STEP

After you've edited your document, check your layout and design one more time during your postwriting step. Use a reader's perspective to make certain that your logic and organization are visually clear. Make certain that your key points are easy to see and follow. If they're not, consider using a different organizational pattern, rephrasing the material, or using different layout and design cues. Of equal importance, remember what didn't work—save yourself editing time on your next document.

SPECIFIC LAYOUT AND DESIGN CONCEPTS

You don't have to become a graphic artist to improve your documents, but understanding basic layout and design concepts can help you plan, edit, and create more successful documents:

Heads and Subheads

Heads and subheads are the visually emphasized words at the start of sections, paragraphs, and topics that are often referred to as L1, L2, L3, L4, and so on. An L1 head is the main or most visually prominent concept in a document. L2, L3, L4, and succeeding subheads are of decreasing (often hierarchical) conceptual importance and visual strength.

Margins and Indents

These need little explanation. Remember that there are, however, left, right, top, and bottom margins, and that indenting material on both the left and right sides can be very effective. Wide margins also allow readers to add notes.

Displayed Lists

Displayed lists are created by simply pulling in the left and right margins around a piece of information. Changing the font, for example, to italic, can add more visual emphasis.

Bullets

Bullets are symbols (e.g., ● ■ □ ☑ ☒ ◆ * ➢ ☒) that are used to show where a piece of information starts or to set off a list. Our recommendation: the simpler, the better.

Font(s) and Typeface(s)

The two most commonly used are some variant of Times New Roman and Helvetica or Arial. Times New Roman is probably the safest choice. Anything too unusual can distract the reader from the message—this includes using all capital letters, all italics, or all boldface.

Integrated Graphics

Graphics are used to simplify information and decrease complex text. They include, among others,

- Tables
- Figures
- Charts

These design cues are important because they allow you to bring consistency and repeating patterns to your work. In addition, they allow you to create *white space*—open places on a page that can help focus your reader's attention.

When you use visual cues, remember to apply them to your headers and footers. Effective headers and footers, especially footers that contain identifying information such as authorship, document title, origination date, computer file name/location, and page numbers, can make a report extremely easy to use and locate in the future.

Applying good layout and design concepts makes it easy for your readers to find what they need and what you want to share.

APPLYING LAYOUT AND DESIGN CONCEPTS IN SAMPLE DOCUMENTS

We have found that simply discussing these concepts is insufficient. Even though people see them every day, many writers find it helpful to see actual before-and-after examples showing how to use these concepts and tools effectively. The figures that follow are designed to illustrate the principles we have described.

Using Bullet Points, White Space, and Inset Margins

Figures 5.3 and 5.4 demonstrate that it is easy to make your key points visually distinct on a page. When you create a document like the memo in Figure 5.3, your readers will be scratching their heads trying to figure out what you want them to know or do. The revised memo in Figure 5.4 should have them nodding in agreement with your points.

When you compare the verbose memo (Figure 5.3) to the revised memo (Figure 5.4), you will notice that both documents have the same audience and goal, and they contain essentially the same information. However, the verbose memo is not only too long, it also lacks the simple visual cues (e.g., bullet points, inset margins, and white space) that focus your attention on key points in the revised memo. It lacks a useful subject

Memo

To: Tom, B-1007 Systems Administrator
From: Ali, Technology Chairperson
Date: November 30, 200x
Subject: Meeting

For our 10:00 am meeting on Friday, December 10, your group
will need to make a decision on which of the following three
options should be implemented for B-1007. The networked systems approach with both Windows NT and AppleTalk, which would
allow us to operate both IBM-compatible and Macintosh units on
the same network, or the networked system approach using just
Windows NT, which would allow us to use the IBM-compatible
units, but not the Macintosh units, or the networked solution using
just AppleTalk, which would not allow us to use IBM-compatible
systems, but which would allow us to use Macintosh systems. We
need to have a decision by the start of the meeting, along with
your decision criteria and the data to support the decision. If you
need additional information, please contact me.

FIGURE 5.3 *Verbose memo with ineffective layout and design.*

Memo—For Your Action

To:	Tom, B-1007 Systems Administrator
From:	Ali, Technology Chairperson
Date:	November 30, 200x
RE:	Agenda 12/10/00 Meeting: Network for B-1007

At our December 10 meeting (10:00, B-1009, Room 105), we
will decide which of three network system options to install in
Building-1007:

- Combined Windows NT and AppleTalk systems
- Windows NT—only system
- AppleTalk-only system

Please bring your group's recommendation and be prepared to discuss your *criteria* and *supporting data,* including

- Requirements
- Time lines
- Costs
- Benefits

If you need additional information, please contact me at x5555.

FIGURE 5.4 *Revised memo with clear layout and design
features.*

line, and, compared to the revised memo, most people would find the original hard to skim. In fact, most people would need to read it several times to understand the main point.

Clear Sections, Subject Lines, Tables, and Heads

Effective, visually and logically consistent memos can also be created by systematically editing your material, adding useful section divisions, heads, figures, charts, or tables. Figures 5.5 and 5.6 illustrate these points. Most readers would find the complex, original memo to be ineffective because it has extensive text and no visual cues to show its organization.

In contrast, the improved memo has a good subject line and is well organized, partially because the integrated table forces the writer to think clearly by providing a structure that organizes ideas and data. The table and the head ("Interpretation of the Data") effectively focus the reader's attention.

To gain the information you need from the original memo (Figure 5.5), you would have to read the entire memo—probably twice. To get the information you need from the improved memo (Figure 5.6) you can simply skim the table. Which memo would you rather receive, and on which memo would you want senior management to find your name?

Layout and Design Concepts with Other Documents

These same concepts apply to e-mail messages, letters, resumes, reports, and proposals. For example, consider the e-mail messages shown in Figures 5.7 and 5.8. They demonstrate that applying these concepts to e-mail adds value, although in many instances, creating a good e-mail message is more difficult than creating a good memo because of the inherent limitations of many e-mail editing packages. Many e-mail packages do not support underlining, bold, or switching of fonts, let alone useful embedding of figures, tables, or graphics. Because of these shortcomings, the writer must write with more clarity and use other visual cues to organize the materials. One effective solution is to use short, well-structured ideas that are broken into short paragraphs with indented margins and lists.

Memo

To: Tom, B-1007 Systems Administrator
From: Ali, Technology Chairperson
Date: December 1, 200x
Subject: Meeting

As you requested, the data that you need to evaluate the appropriateness of the three different networks for B-1007 is available from our last inventory. We showed that we had 120 Macintosh systems, as of Q1, 199x. We had 85 Macintosh systems in Q2 of 199x and we will probably have 50 Macintosh systems by Q1 of 2002. The number of Macintosh systems is being decreased systematically.

We also showed in our last inventory that we had 150 and 185 IBM-compatible systems in Q1 and Q2 of 199x, respectively. We are also projecting systematically increasing the number of IBM-compatible systems, directly equal in number to the number of Macintosh systems decreased, resulting in a net number of 240 IBM-compatibles in Q1 of 2002.

If you need more information, please contact me at x5555.

FIGURE 5.5 *Complex memo lacking visual cues.*

Memo

To: Tom, B-1007 Systems Administrator
From: Ali, Technology Chairperson
Date: December 1, 200x
RE: Data for 12/10/0x Meeting on Systems Decision for B-1007

As you requested, the data that you need to evaluate the appropriateness of the three different networks for B-1007 is summarized in Table 1 from our last inventory.

System Type	Q1 200x	Q2 200x	Q1 2002
Macintosh	120	85	50
IBM-Compat.	150	185	240

Table 1: Actual and Projected Systems for B-1007

Interpretation of the Data. Table 1 shows that we currently have large numbers of both IBM-compatible and Macintosh systems, and although we are decreasing the number of Macintosh machines, a mixture of system types is projected to continue through *Q1 of 2002.* If you need more information, please contact me at x5555.

FIGURE 5.6 *Improved memo using a table and head.*

To: RD TaSpar
From: Ron Hein <ron@eznet.net>
Date: Portfolio analysis
cc:

Your last e-mail requested information on how I would like to balance my retirement portfolio. My preference is to use a combination of the S&P 500 stock index fund that you recommended, one-year Jumbo CDs, the Colorado oil and gas leases I currently hold, the non-callable 10-year corporate bonds, the international growth funds with a German focus, and the individual stocks (Lucent, Xerox, and Cisco). I am not interested in holding any of my current Internet stocks, including Amazon.com, for the long term.

Proportionately, I would like to have my holdings divided 25%, 10%, 5%, 15%, 10%, and 15%, 10%, and 10%.

Please give me your feedback.

FIGURE 5.7 *Common e-mail layout using only ASCII characters and no visual cues.*

To: RD TaSpar
From: Ron Hein <ron@eznet.net>
Date: Portfolio analysis
cc:

Your October 5 e-mail requested information on how I would like to balance my retirement portfolio.

1) My preference, as we discussed, is to hold the following combination of investments:

>S&P 500 stock index fund	25%
>One-year Jumbo CDs	10%
>Colorado oil and gas leases (current holdings)	05%
>Non-callable 10-year corporate bonds	15%
>International growth funds (German focus)	10%
>Lucent	15%
>Xerox	10%
>Cisco	10%

2) Sell my current Internet stocks, including Amazon.com.

I anticipate that you will complete these changes by 3:00 today. Please call if you have concerns or when you have completed the transactions.

FIGURE 5.8 *Improved e-mail layout using only ASCII characters and indents.*

Michael T. C. Jones
2250 S. Vine St. Denver, Colorado 80222
(303)555-1234

EDUCATION
University of Chicago   200x
M.B.A., Finance
University of Denver   1998
B.A., Mathematics

EXPERIENCE
Franklin Securities, NY, NY   1999–200x
Assistant Director of Finance
Successfully evaluated and restructured
Bond Division by developing creative
financing; increased profits 140%. Created
financial system; decreased staffing 25%.

BDA Associates, NY, NY   1998–1999
Senior Financial Analyst
Developed creative, integrated solutions to
financial problems and resolved mathematically based resource allocation problems.

WORKSHOPS/INSERVICE TRAINING
Took workshops on Writing Financial Proposals, TQM Processes, and Teamwork.

COMPUTER EXPERIENCE
Familiar with Windows NT, System 7+, UNIX,
Bloomberg, Lotus 1-2-3, Microsoft Office
(Access, Excel, PowerPoint), and C++

FIGURE 5.9 *Sample resume with few design features.*

Use Layout and Design Ideas with Your Resumes

When you want to move up in your organization or to
find a new job, remember to use layout and design
ideas and tools with your resume. As the resumes in
Figures 5.9 and 5.10 demonstrate, using layout and
design cues can improve the visual organization of a
document by reducing hard-to-read blocks of text.
Resumes are often given only a minute or two of a
manager's time, so they need to make an immediate,
positive impact. They are seldom read for pleasure—
especially when the manager takes them home to read
in the evenings or on weekends!

END POINT

Common layout and design tools can help you improve
documents to get the results you need. Using tables and
figures can be especially effective in simplifying infor-

MICHAEL T. C. JONES
2250 S. Vine St. • Denver, Colorado 80222 • (303)555-1234

EDUCATION

University of Chicago, Chicago, Illinois   June 200x
M.B.A., Finance

University of Denver, Denver, Colorado   May 1998
B.A., Mathematics

EXPERIENCE

Franklin Securities. New York City   1999–200x
Assistant Director of Finance

- Successfully evaluated and restructured Bond Division.
- Developed creative financing that increased profits 140%.
- Created a financial system that decreased staffing 25%.

BDA Associates. New York City   1998–1999
Senior Financial Analyst

- Developed creative, integrated solutions to complex financial problems.
- Produced effective solutions to mathematically based resource-allocation problems.

WORKSHOPS/INSERVICE TRAINING

- Writing Financial Proposals, TQM Processes, Teamwork

COMPUTER EXPERIENCE

- Windows NT, System 7+, Unix
- Bloomberg
- Lotus 1-2-3
- Microsoft Office (Word, Access, Excel, PowerPoint)
- C++

FIGURE 5.10 *Sample resume with multiple design features.*

mation and advancing arguments. As you move through the writing and editing process, it is crucial that you consider the look of your documents as a way to visually reinforce your written word.

Making Your E-mail Go Further and Do More

E-mail is playing an increasingly important role in business communication, with tens of millions of pieces of mail being transmitted daily. In 1998, the Electronic Messaging Association (http://www.emailhelp.com/ema .html) estimated that by the year 2000, users will send approximately 6 trillion electronic messages. Forrester Research (http://emailhelp.com/forrester.html), in a 1996 report titled "People and Technology Strategies," estimated that 60 million Americans were exchanging e-mail and that the use of e-mail would grow tenfold over the next five years. Elsewhere, Kate Delhagen of Forrester Research noted (in 1998) that e-mail has exploded over the last five years and that within 10 years, over 80 percent of the U.S. population will have an e-mail address.[1]

E-mail is also becoming a problematic form of business communication because of barriers that exist at both the company and individual user levels:

- A lack of common standards and expectations (etiquette) among users

- A need for universally supported software/formatting features

- Security questions (internal, external, encryption)

- Increasing concerns about the document life cycle of e-mail

In addition to the material in this chapter, useful and regularly updated information is available about these and other e-mail topics at various web sites, some of which are cited in Table 6.1. Regularly updated infor-

TABLE 6.1 E-MAIL SOURCES

E-mail, Internet Issue	Web Site	Web Site
E-mail growth	emailhelp.com/email-ed.html	emailhelp.com/forrester.html	emailhelp.com/ema.html
E-mail etiquette/issues	albion.com/netiquette/book/index.html	iwillfollow.com/emailetiquette.html	everythingemail.net
E-mail glossary/emoticons	newbie.net/jumpstations/SmileyFAQ.html	windweaver.com/emoticon.htm	everythingemail.net/glossary.html
E-mail style and layout	albion.com/netiquette/book/index.html	webfoot.com/advice/email.top.html	
Business etiquette International etiquette	bspage.com/1netiq/netiq.html	newbie.net	
Ethics	fau.edu/rinaldi/net/index.html	newbie.net	

mation will be extremely valuable because of the rapidly evolving nature of this field.

LACK OF COMMON STANDARDS AND EXPECTATIONS

There are no commonly accepted standards for e-mail that are parallel, for example, to those for business letters. Writers who have style questions about business letters and documents can quickly check commonly available references, such as *The Prentice-Hall Style Manual* (Mary A. DeVries, Prentice Hall, 1992), *The Chicago Manual of Style,* 14th edition (Editors, University of Chicago Press, 1993), or *The Gregg Reference Manual,* 7th edition (William A Sabin, Macmillan/McGraw-Hill, 1994). However, guidelines for e-mail are less common and less widely circulated.

This is changing, but the problem of accepted standards remains. Perhaps the best-known and most widely accepted source for standards is *Netiquette* by Virginia Shea, which is available both in hard copy and on-line (http://www.albion.com/netiquette/book/index.html).

MAXIMIZING E-MAIL COMMUNICATION

Be sure your e-mail messages carry the impact to get the recipients' attention and achieve your intended goal. Table 6.2 details some frequently encountered problems of e-mail and links them to the writing and editing process. Whether it's making your subject line too vague or forgetting to spell check, you can maximize communication and avoid pitfalls by keeping the writing and editing process in mind when you create e-mail.

Here is a brief overview of common e-mail problems and some recommendations to help solve them. Refer to Appendix A for sample e-mail documents to illustrate these points.

Subject Lines

Missing or uninformative subject lines are a problem for e-mail senders and readers. Subject lines for e-mail, as for memos, are intended to focus both the sender and the reader: The sender can check the subject line to see if the goal of a memo was met, and the reader can decide when, or whether, to open the incoming message.

Recommendation: Use subject lines that are concise and informative and that highlight the goal of the message or a needed action.

TABLE 6.2 E-MAIL PROBLEMS LINKED TO A WRITING AND EDITING PROCESS

Individual User E-mail Issues	Prewriting	Drafting	Editing Logic	Editing Layout	Editing Grammar	Postwriting
Missing/poor subject line						X
Weak structure/ organization	X		X			
Too much information	X	X	X			X
No attachments	X		X			
Unusable attachments	X					X
Sloppy work			X	X	X	
No spell check					X	X
All caps	X				X	X
No caps	X				X	X
Visual cues				X		X
No visual cues				X		X
Getting too fancy				X		X
Emotives				X		X
Oops, I sent it!						X
Paper trail	X		X			X
Copying the world	X		X			X
Forwarding to the world	X		X			X

Weak Structure or Organization

KEY CONCEPT

Early users of e-mail simply dashed off notes and forgot about them, causing bad habits to develop among generations of e-mail users. Those bad habits are proliferating as e-mail becomes the preferred method of correspondence. Some companies, such as Microsoft, pride themselves on their extensive, if not exclusive, use of e-mail for internal correspondence. Unfortunately, many people don't take the time and care with e-mail messages that they might with a hard-copy memo or business letter. This leads to ineffective messages that require more follow-up for clarification and response.

Recommendation: Spend the same amount of time in the writing and editing process drafting and editing e-mail as you would memos and letters.

Too Much Information

KEY CONCEPT

One of the most frustrating problems facing e-mail users is how to impart a lot of information.

When you have a long (multiple paragraphs or pages) message, it can be helpful to use attachments to reduce the size of the e-mail to make the information less intimidating and more user-friendly. However, especially for cross-company and cross-platform (UNIX versus Mac versus Windows) document exchanges, it is often difficult to know if the receiver will be able to open the attachments that you want to include. For example, if you want to summarize a page of text by using a table or graphic, will the receiver's e-mail or other software open it?

Recommendation: Before you send e-mail attachments, verify that the receiver has the ability to open and use them. It is often preferable to avoid software-specific file formats (such as Microsoft's .doc files) and to instead use formats that can be interpreted by multiple software packages (such as .rtf).

 Just Sloppy

Sloppy work is an increasing problem as more people begin to use e-mail. Common failures include the following:

- Not knowing the goal of an e-mail
- Treating an e-mail more as a conversation than as a concise memo
- Failing to develop logical transitions among ideas
- Not using a spell checker
- Using poor typing habits

Using ALL CAPS or no capitalization can eliminate cues that readers unconsciously use to recognize the visual patterns (outlines) of words. These types of errors are often made by users who lack basic keyboarding/typing skills and by users who try to hide their lack of grammar skills (albeit, unsuccessfully).

The problem of sloppy work is briefly addressed in "A Beginner's Guide to Effective Email, revision 2.0" by Kaitlin Duck Sherwood (http://webfoot.com/advice/email.top.html). Sherwood indicates that e-mail is often viewed as being more conversational than traditional paper-based media and that, as a result, e-mail tends to be sloppier than communication on paper.

Recommendation: Reread your e-mail message before you send it. Avoid being sloppy. Sloppy errors can create significant liabilities. As a case in point, embarrassing e-mail often gets forwarded to others without the sender's permission. Use the editing and postwriting substeps from Chapter 3 to decrease sloppy errors. You risk embarrassment if you send out an e-mail before editing or proofreading it.

Visual Cues

A multitude of visual cues can help make your e-mail messages easier to read. Unfortunately, senders frequently don't know if the receiver's software will support (interpret) the codes that are used to represent those visual cues in the document. Many times, the visual cues (bolding, margin changes, italics, color, etc.) end up as embedded gibberish in the receiver's document. This is because many e-mail programs support only a basic ASCII code set instead of extended or special-character sets. In her "Beginner's Guide to Effective Email," Sherwood offers a useful overview of some of the barriers to effective formatting of text materials.

Recommendation: If you are sending e-mail to specific individuals on a regular basis, send a test message to verify whether the receiver's software can interpret your embedded formatting. If your e-mail message is a one-off document, play it safe and use simple, straight text or ASCII characters; don't try to get fancy. Instead, focus on writing materials that are well organized, go straight to the point, use good transitions, and use numbered or lettered points and line spacing as visual cues.

 Getting Too Fancy

For many e-mail users, the fundamental goal is quick, concise communication. Spending too much time creating a fancy document is wasted effort, especially when the e-mail is just to let a colleague know that you going to a 30-minute meeting.

Recommendation: Match your effort to the importance of your message. Use visual cues, but first know what you need to say, say it clearly, and then stop.

 Emoticons

You've no doubt seen little "smiley" faces embedded in e-mail messages:

:-)   ;-)   :-(

They're cute, but cute doesn't necessarily fit in a business message. In addition, unless you and the receiver use a "smiley" web site (http://www.mindweaver.com/emoticon.htm or newbies.net) to understand their meaning, those little cues can have mixed messages. For example, you might be tempted to use the emoticon :-X with a new client who asks you to guarantee nondisclosure. Unfortunately, :-X can mean "my lips are sealed," or it can mean "a big wet kiss."

Recommendation: Avoid using emoticons and smileys except for casual messages to colleagues you know extremely well or to friends. Emoticons seldom add value to business correspondence, and they can be counterproductive.

Oops, I Sent It!

There are hundreds of horror stories involving e-mail messages that never should have been created or sent. In many recent cases of litigation—for example, those related to tobacco, silicon breast implants, automobiles, and software—individuals have created paper trails that have greatly helped litigants. For an example of problems associated with e-mail, check out the article about Microsoft in *Newsweek:* "When e-mail bites back" (November 23, 1998, pages 45–46), which can be accessed at www.newsweek.com.

Forwarding E-mail and Copying the World

Two chief caveats: Do not copy the world or forward e-mail to everyone. It is all too easy to send trivial e-mail to dozens of people by using distribution lists rather than targeting appropriate individuals. The reverse is also true: It is easy for those receiving e-mail to forward it, intentionally or unintentionally, to a multitude of others—perhaps including individuals whom the original sender deliberately excluded.

Recommendation: Complete your postwriting step before you let your finger hit the Return key or click the mouse. Decide whether you might better send the material by conventional mail or discuss it in a phone call. Decide who should receive the material and establish a document cycle for the message (for example, read and delete, do not distribute, etc.).

Nonstandard Formatting Features

One of the problems facing both individual users and companies is the lack of universally supported software features. For the purposes of this discussion, we are defining software features as those that provide various text-emphasis techniques, such as margins or indents, bolding, italics, underlining, color, inserted figures or graphics, attachments, and so forth.

Formatting features become a problem when, for example, a person sends an e-mail to a receiver at another company or at another branch of the same company. Depending on the software package being used (and in some cases the service provider), the sender doesn't know whether the e-mail will be readable by the receiver. It may be filled with gibberish. The response may read *?#$%?*&???—or there may be no response at all!

Recommendation: At a company level, make certain you adopt a commonly used and widely supported e-mail package that allows for the formatting of text. At the individual level, verify that the e-mail capabilities of key contacts are compatible with yours.

SECURITY CONCERNS

One of the problems that is being faced by many business users is the question of security, especially with content-sensitive materials being sent out over the Internet. At the company level, data security (internal and external) and encryption are vital to consider.

Recommendation: Companies need to establish protocols dealing not only with the use of encryption software, but also with the integrity and protection of the e-mail/server system from external and internal threats. Companies need to address the practical problems that can result from a failure to screen for viruses, and they need to protect against hackers and unauthorized access to systems, software, and documents. Valuable ideas on security and data encryption are available at the Electronic Messaging Association web site (http://www.ema.org/ema-home.htm), at www.newbies.net, and at the following sites for Pretty Good Privacy (PGP):

http://www.web.mit.edu/network/pgp.html

http://www.nai.com/products/security/security.asp

http://www.thegate.gamers.org/~tony/pgp.html

DOCUMENT LIFE CYCLE OF E-MAIL

The explosion in the use of e-mail has led to the creation of massive numbers of documents that do not have a defined life cycle. They are often not destroyed by the sender or the receiver and, in fact, are stored permanently due to the archiving practices of computer support groups.

Recommendation: As part of their document management policies, companies need to establish document life-cycle procedures to ensure that critical documents (such as patent information) are retained and that other documents having potentially negative legal implications are appropriately handled. In addition, companies need to establish access restrictions for users to ensure that only authorized users can view or alter documents. For a more extensive discussion of document management, see Chapter 2.

END POINT

E-mail is fast becoming a mandatory means of communicating in the business world. In the very near future, the vast majority of families in the United States are expected to have e-mail addresses. The use of e-mail to communicate effectively, to reduce meetings, and to save time and money on both local and international levels cannot be ignored. Spend time learning how to improve your e-mail messages and how to use this means of communication more effectively. In the long run, you'll save time and money—and produce the results you want.

CHAPTER 7

Memos

Managers and executives write so many memos in the course of the day that they seldom stop to think about the characteristics of a good memo. Their goal, quite often, is to get the memo written and check that task off their to-do list. This can create problems, especially when the writers have not made a habit of using a writing and editing process or when they skip some of the writing and editing steps.

Writing good memos can be a fairly simple task when the writing and editing process is consistently used. In this chapter, we examine some of the factors that increase the chances your memo will be read and acted upon, and we offer tips for improving the content and design of your memos.

Many of the concepts that we discuss throughout Part 2 (logic, structure, organization, layout and design, and grammar) apply to multiple types of documents, because the requirements and goals are often overlapping. You can easily recognize and use those overlaps to save time by applying similar "solutions" to seemingly different products.

GOOD MEMOS ARE READ AND ACTED UPON

What factors increase the likelihood that a manager or executive will read and act upon what you've written? We asked the people who do it every day.

During writing workshops, we frequently ask executives to review copies of actual corporate memos, e-mail messages, letters, and reports to determine what characteristics influence whether they will read a document. Their preferences are:

- Short documents
- Documents from their bosses
- Documents clearly linked to a context or requirement
- Memos with good subject lines and/or first paragraphs (or with reports, introductions, or executive summaries)
- Well-organized materials
- Documents that are concisely phrased, well written, easy to read, and have appropriate tone
- Documents with heads, subheads, bullets, and figures—documents they can skim
- Documents that have a nice font and aren't jammed onto a page
- Very short documents!

Additionally, managers and executives indicate that they generally ignore memos, letters, and reports that are:

- Long
- Hard to skim
- Hard to understand, difficult to read, or poorly written
- Unprofessional in appearance

This implies that you should create memos and e-mail that:

- Are short
- Have clear objectives and subject lines
- Are well organized
- Have visual cues to the organization
- Use sufficient supporting data
- Are clear and concise

KEY CONCEPT — CREATING GOOD MEMOS

It's easy to improve memos by applying the following quick-and-easy suggestions:

- *Have the right content:* Define your objective and analyze your audience (see Chapters 11 and 12) to be sure you meet the needs of your readers and your own purpose in writing the memo.
- *Avoid excessive detail:* Make it easy on your readers to do their work by including only what is needed— don't write novels!
- *Write a memo readers can skim:* Use good organizational cues and visual design so your readers don't have to read every word you write.

A Changing Distinction between Memos and E-mail

Traditionally, there has been a very simple dichotomy between memos and business letters. Memos have been internal documents and business letters have been external documents.

That distinction of internal and external documents has become blurred as we all begin to use e-mail—for internal and external communication—more frequently.

This is good, but can also be problematic. It's good if it leads to quicker and less complicated communication. It can be problematic when people fail to realize that their e-mailed memos are not internal documents that are automatically confidential or protected or limited in circulation.

When memos are sent as e-mails to people outside of a company (i.e., external documents), they functionally become business letters, and consequently they must be held to a higher standard during all phases of their creation, editing, distribution, and life cycle. Once you send out a business letter or an e-mail, that message is no longer under your control. As a result, you need to pay more attention to your prewriting, editing, and postwriting processes.

In addition, the following suggestions from Charles Brusaw, et al., in *The Business Writer's Handbook*[1] can be very helpful. According to Brusaw, when writing memos, you should do the following:

- Use meaningful subject lines that convey the essence of the memo.
- Use a check-off line for ☑ action, ☑ information, or ☑ response.
- Write clear, focused, and forthright memos. (Don't tell a story.)
- Put your recommendations and key points up front.
- Use useful, concise, supporting detail.
- Use informative, visually sequenced heads and subheads.
- Use lists and bullets.
- Use a personal tone.

The late Malcolm Forbes[2] also made a number of excellent suggestions on how to write good memos and letters:

- Know what you want; state it in one sentence.
- Plunge right in; give the purpose of the letter in the first paragraph.
- Write so it's enjoyable; use a reader's viewpoint; be natural; be positive.

- Give it your best; make it visually appealing; make it short; emphasize your points.
- State what you're going to do; state what you want done. Sum it up and get out.

KEY CONCEPT SAMPLE MEMOS

Many people love to use templates to design their documents. Most word processors now offer style sheet options that include pull-down boxes with pre-designed heads and subheads. These are very useful, and they can be even more useful when you use those heads and subheads to emphasize your organization, your logic, and the structure of your messages. To help you visualize how to improve memos (and e-mail), we provide sample memos in Appendixes C and D that show common problems and effective solutions. Review these samples to help you identify how you and your team can strengthen documents.

Consider the sample memos in Figures 7.1 to 7.4. The first memo (Figure 7.1) is poorly organized and written. The second (Figure 7.2) is a revision, which is both well organized and well written, but illustrates that the effort spent to create an artificially precise memo is not always the way to handle the task. Calling

---

INTERNAL MEMORANDUM

To: Bobby
From: Jim
Date: August 1st

Per our discussion of June 10th, I've been thinking about those books we were talking about. I think that that one you showed me with the orange cover would be a pretty good one. Why don't you get me a copy of it. That Words into type book was pretty good, too. Really liked paperback one, *Hire Me!* by that guy Powell Randell.

I think I'd like a copy of those two. I need them for next week's meeting. Thank you in advance. What was the other one I liked? The Handbook of Business Writing? Get one of those for me, if you can. I need it for next week's meeting. Thank you in advance. What was the other one I liked? The Handbook of Business Writing? Get one of those for me, if you can.

FIGURE 7.1 *A poorly written memo with muddled organization. Can you afford to send it?*

MEMO

To:	Bobby
From:	Jim
Date:	August 1, 1999
Subject:	Writing books to be ordered
	☒ For Your Action

Please order one copy of each of the following books:

(a) Brusaw, Charles T., Alred, Gerald J., and Oliu, Walter E. *The Business Writer's Handbook,* 4th edition. New York: St. Martin's Press, 1993. [ISBN: 0-312-05734-2]

(b) DiGaetani, John L. (editor) *The Handbook of Executive Communication.* Homewood, Illinois: Dow Jones-Irwin, 1986. [ISBN: 0-87094-2]

(c) Powell, C. Randall. *Career Planning Today: Hire Me!,* 2nd edition.

(d) *Words into Type,* 3rd edition. Englewood Cliffs, New Jersey: Prentice-Hall, 1974. [ISBN: 0-13-964262-5]

I need them by August 15. To save time, you might order from Total Information, 844 Dewey; try either (716) 254-0621 or their 800 number: (800) 876-4637. If you order using our credit card number, they will ship the items directly to us—no additional charge. Thanks.

FIGURE 7.2 *Revised memo with excellent organization and visual cues. But can you afford the time to write it? It may be faster to order via the Internet, for example.*

MEMO (VIA E-MAIL)

Date: Wednesday, 06 Jan 1999, 13:03
To: AA1234@hotmail.com
From: Ron Hein <ron@eznet.net>
Subject: Re: price list please

Thank you for your inquiry. Our prices vary with the type and complexity of work that you need done and your timelines. As you may have noticed on our web page, we offer services including creating resumes and employment materials, editing academic materials, editing manuals and reports, authoring original materials, and delivering training seminars.

Because of the diverse nature of our services and the varying skills needed to complete different projects, we quote projects on an individual basis. The easiest way for us to quote a project is if you can send us some information on what you need done, including sample pages, or give us a call and we can talk.

Ron Hein
January 6, 1999

Phone: (716) 671-6170
Fax: (716) 255-4008
E-mail: ron@eznet.net
Internet: ron-hein.com

FIGURE 7.3 *Memo with no visual cues.*

MEMO (VIA E-MAIL)

Date: Wednesday, 06 Jan 1999, 13:03
To: AA1234@hotmail.com
From: Ron Hein <ron@eznet.net>
Subject: Re: price list please

Hello Todd—

Thank you for your inquiry. Our prices vary with the type and complexity of work that you need done and your timelines.

As you may have noticed on our web page, we offer services that include

- creating resumes and employment materials
- editing academic materials
- editing manuals and reports
- authoring original materials
- delivering training seminars

Because of the diverse nature of our services and the varying skills needed to complete different projects, we quote projects on an individual basis.

Next Steps. The easiest way for us to quote a project is if you can send us some information on what you need done, including sample pages, or give us a call and we can talk.

Thanks.

Ron Hein
January 6, 1999

Phone: (716) 671-6170
Fax: (716) 255-4008
E-mail: ron@eznet.net
Internet: ron-hein.com

FIGURE 7.4 *Revised memo with simple visual cues—a bulleted list and a subhead.*

the bookstore, or using the Internet (amazon.com or barnesandnoble.com), for example, would be a quicker and easier solution than drafting, revising, and following up with another memo.

Figures 7.3 to 7.4 illustrate how memos that are sent as e-mail can be quickly and easily improved by adding simple visual cues, such as lists, bullet points, and subheads that indicate the next action to be taken.

END POINT

Memos are becoming more widely used with the advent of e-mail. Memos, which traditionally were internal documents, are being transformed into external documents that replace more traditional business letters. Because of that, it is important to use both document management systems (Chapter 2) and writing and editing processes (Chapter 3) to ensure that the content is appropriate and will not lead to legal liability. Further, the use of a writing and editing process can ensure that memos incorporate appropriate organizational plans and visual cues that make them easier to create and to read.

Business Letters

Business letters are an important link to individuals and groups outside of your company. While written communication within a company is generally done through e-mail and memos, business letters are generally thought of as a more formal means of communicating with those outside of a company.

In this chapter, we discuss the use of writing and editing processes to avoid common errors in writing business letters.

We will help you improve your writing and editing processes, and thus the quality of your products, by examining five factors that help determine the success of business letters:

- Content
- Organization
- Tone and phrasing
- Correctly spelled names and titles
- Style—layout and design

CONTENT

Most writers assume that they automatically put the appropriate content in their letters. In reality, that is often a bad assumption, which is why the writing and editing process (Chapter 3) contains a *prewriting step,* which includes analyzing your readers, and a *postwriting step,* in which you confirm that your content coincides with your goals.

Valuable Letter-Writing Resources

For those of you with limited experience in writing everyday business letters, a number of excellent resources are available. Sabin, *The Gregg Reference Manual,*[1] 7th edition, covers correspondence and usage issues in extensive detail, as does DeVries in *The Prentice-Hall Style Manual.*[2] Both books contain hundreds of pages of sample documents and illustrations showing how to handle the minute details involved in creating technically correct correspondence.

The first step (prewriting) will help you determine who will be reading your material, what they know, what they want to know, what you want them to do or not do, and how to give them the information they need. The last step (postwriting) will help ensure that you have met your objectives and avoided fatal errors.

One of the more effective additions to a business letter is an *action statement:* an indication of what you are going to do next or what you expect the reader to do. An action statement can be effective as a first sentence or a closing sentence.

 ORGANIZATION

Making sure your business letter is organized is a given, yet many overlook this crucial step, and the resulting letter resembles a rambling stroll though the countryside.

To create a well-organized business letter, it is especially useful to apply the ideas suggested in Chapter 4 on logic, structure, and organizational plans. If your ideas fit into a problem-solution format, then organize your letter in that mode. If you can talk effectively about your ideas in relation to time (e.g., fiscal quarters) or geographic or market areas, and that perspective will help your reader better understand the implications, then organize your letter (or a section of it) accordingly.

When you use organizational plans to help your readers see the pertinence of your ideas and to make your ideas more familiar, you will decrease their work and increase the likelihood that they will be able to assimilate your points.

Apply the ideas of Malcolm Forbes[3]:

- Know where you are going.
- Make your main point in the first sentence or paragraph.
- Use clear, concise, straightforward statements.
- Sum up.
- Get out.

Forbes's advice is excellent. You need to put your reason for writing in your first sentence or paragraph. It is sometimes recommended that you put good news in your first sentence, and if you have bad news, to buffer it by using a neutral first sentence or paragraph. For example, "We have greatly enjoyed being able to supply your company with high-quality parts for the last five years. But we can no longer supply parts to your company, as your account is 90 days past due." This technique can be problematic, however, because many people skip the buffer and go directly to the bad news. Use the buffer cautiously.

TONE AND PHRASING

KEY CONCEPT

Tone is another one of those commonsense points that is often overlooked. In seminars, one of the best exercises we do is to pass out a sample letter and ask for a show of hands: Would you read this, set it aside for later, or toss it? Tone errors are the second most common reason (after too much information with no visual cues) that managers and executives give for setting aside a document to read later.

DANGER!

Tone errors often reflect poor editing for grammar and failing to complete the postwriting step. Tone errors often result from anger. If you write a letter when you are angry, don't mail it immediately. Put it into a desk drawer, let it sit overnight, and then review it in the morning. It's easier and more effective to take the time to review it than to have to apologize or to suffer the consequences of your poor judgment.

Tone Errors Include Negative Phrasing

Some letter writers will take a negative approach:

We understand your customers have been canceling contracts due to your inability to meet milling tolerances of ±0.001 microns.

Building on a positive statement is usually much more effective:

*Our new CNC machines are helping our cus-
tomers meet strict milling tolerances of ±0.001
microns and increase market share.*

Often, the wrong tone is a result of one or two words
that convey the wrong impression. Other times, tone
errors are more problematic because they reflect a
writer's basic personality, which is hard to hide in your
writing.

Because it is difficult to take on the reader's perspective
and to recognize the "wrong" tone in a letter that you
have written, we strongly recommend using a
postwriting step that includes letting your letter sit
overnight and then rereading it or, better yet, asking a
colleague to read it before you send it out.

Other Phrasing Concerns

Some phrasing errors occur as a result of being
immersed in a company's culture. These include the
excessive use of jargon and acronyms, gender-specific
phrasing, trite phrases, and using the passive voice.

Jargon and Acronyms

How do you know you're using too much jargon and
too many acronyms? One clue is writing that appears
codelike: ". . . the SLC group at EK is very concerned
about JIT delivery and ROE for the L&D function of the
CNC . . ." When the spell checker for your word processor highlights every third word, it's time to start editing.

Gender-Specific Language

Not only is gender-specific language typically inaccu-
rate, it is often inappropriate and can even cause legal
problems. For example, do you mean security men or
security officers? Managers, men who . . . or individuals
who . . . ? Senior vice presidents, women who . . . or
senior vice presidents, executives who . . . ? If a specific
group is composed of only one gender, it is appropriate
to note it; however, it is probably not appropriate, at
least in the United States, to suggest that gender pre-
cludes employment in certain positions.

Trite Phrases

Trite phrases such as "Have a nice day" do not belong
in business letters.

Active and Passive Sentence Construction

Phrasing problems can also be related to active versus
passive voice in sentence construction. In general, use
concise, active voice. It is shorter, eliminates a percep-

tion of overly formal writing, and increases the effectiveness of your writing.

Carol Gelderman in her chapter, "Business Letters,"[4] provides an excellent illustration of the difference between active-versus-passive construction and verb tenses—two concepts that are frequently confused. As Gelderman illustrates, it is easy to write both active and passive constructions in all verb tenses:

> *When you use active voice, the subject "does" the action of the verb:*
> - *Smith writes the best letter. (active, present tense)*
> - *Smith wrote the best letter. (active, past tense)*
> - *Smith will write the best letter. (active, future tense)*
>
> *When you use passive voice, the subject is "acted upon" by something else:*
> - *The best letter is written by Smith. (passive, present tense)*
> - *The best letter was written by Smith. (passive, past tense)*
> - *The best letter will be written by Smith. (passive, future tense)*

Using the active voice in your business letters will significantly shorten them and often make them more effective. The passive voice is only effective if you want to maintain a formal tone.

CORRECTLY SPELLED NAMES AND TITLES

Do people work for Proctor and Gamble or Procter & Gamble? Is your potential client Kathy Smith, Cathy Smithe, Kathryn Smith, or Ms. Kaye Smith? One of the quickest ways to lose the confidence of someone with whom you hope to do business is to misspell that company's or individual's name. It shows you don't care enough to hunt through files, check a web site, or make a phone call. Remember, it's always worth taking the time to confirm the spelling of proper names.

A fatal error that ranks close to misspelling a person's name or a company name is giving someone the wrong title—be it too high or too low. We guarantee that if Ms. K. Smith is a senior manager and you refer to her as a senior vice president, Ms. Smith won't be impressed—it might even remind her that a glass ceiling prevents her from becoming a senior vice president!

There is often more than one way to use titles correctly. For guidelines, we suggest using *The New York*

Times Manual of Style[5] and the *Chicago Manual of Style,*[6] as well as visiting web sites. For example, we recently needed to know how to use certain honorary titles in Japan. The answer was simply a web site away (the Japanese Embassy).

Avoiding Fatal Errors

Fatal errors like misspelling someone's name or using the wrong title can be avoided by making a quick phone call, checking other correspondence, or logging on to a web site and checking your information. If you're lucky, you might make direct contact with the person you need to deal with—perhaps eliminating the need for your letter or making it a follow-up or confirmation letter instead.

STYLE—LAYOUT AND DESIGN

Creating effective business letters requires more effort—and more writing and editing skill—than creating effective memos. We say this because writers often use visual cues in memos to help them overcome poor writing and organizational skills and to make their logic and organization easy to see and follow.

In contrast, some people feel that they should not use visual cues in business letters. They think that managers and executives aren't used to seeing such cues and that they are negatively perceived.

Eight Deadly Cover Letter Errors

Michelle Magee, formerly Assistant Director of Placement at the University of Rochester's Simon School of Business, in her seminars on cover letters, often discussed eight deadly errors that need to be avoided:

- Typographical errors
- Gross grammatical errors
- Misspelled company or employer names
- Content that lacks substance
- Content that doesn't sell
- Templated or form letter content
- Wrong company name (often due to form letters)
- Sloppy, crumpled, coffee-stained letters with handmade corrections

Michelle Magee is now the Program Coordinator for the Office of Cooperative Education and Career Services at Rochester Institute of Technology.

However, when we ask managers and executives in our seminars whether they prefer to receive business letters with or without visual cues (subheads, displayed or bulleted lists, indented margins, subject lines, etc.) to make the key points easier to read, the vast majority— 90 percent in a typical seminar—say they prefer receiving business letters that contain visual cues. Why? Easy. It takes too much time to scan a traditional letter to decide what you need to do with it. They don't have any more free time to read business letters than they do to read memos and e-mail, so anything you can do to facilitate their work is a plus.

Unless you are dealing with a very conservative reader (figure this out during your prewriting step), use visual cues (subheads, displayed or bulleted lists, indented margins, subject lines, etc.) to make your letters easier to read.

END POINT

In a business letter, it is important to verify that you have included the right content, used an appropriate organizational pattern, avoided errors in tone and phrasing, spelled names and titles correctly, and used style and layout and design features that make your letters easy to read. The sample letters included in Appendix D illustrate solutions to such concerns.

Reports and Executive Summaries

If you're new to report writing, the task may seem formidable. However, most of us have had experience writing academic reports, and you may be relieved to learn that business and academic reports share many of the same processes, such as prewriting, editing, and postwriting. Further, these characteristics can be linked to the writing and editing steps, as shown in Figures 9.1 and 9.2.

In this chapter, we discuss how a writing and editing process can help you improve your reports and save time. We also review how to avoid specific report-writing problems and pitfalls, how to integrate tables and figures to advance your arguments, and how to maximize the use of executive summaries.

KEY CONCEPT — WHAT MAKES A GOOD REPORT?

Before we begin to discuss process, it will be helpful to review the characteristics of good business reports. Table 9.1 describes the basic characteristics of a useful report:

- Clear structure
- Ease of use
- Visual cues
- Well written and edited
- Short format

Report Characteristics	Business	Academic
Are Written to Meet Needs of Specific Users/ Decision Makers	✓	✓
Have an executive summary that helps users make decisions	✓	Varies
Define problem(s) and recommendation(s) up front	Varies	Varies
Are focused, brief, and accurate	✓	✓
Are functional (inform, document, evaluate and/or persuade)	✓	✓
Identify/Justify Assumptions and Opinions	✓	✓
Avoid unintentional bias and distortions of fact and logic	✓	✓
Use "Company/Group" Standards for Document Layout/Design	✓	✓
Use consistent layout/design to show structure/relationships	✓	✓
Use fonts, heads, and subheads to facilitate understanding	✓	✓
Use figures/tables/charts to advance/support key points	✓	✓
Provide needed references, footnotes, and in-text citations	✓	✓
Require Coordination and Teamwork	Often	Varies
Improved by discussions/negotiations of content	✓	✓
Are prepared under tight deadlines and due dates	✓	✓
Are often integrated with other reports (within/across areas)	Often	Seldom
Are periodically (quarterly, annually) revised/updated	Often	Seldom
Are presented and discussed/defended in meetings	Often	Some
Are Planned and Edited for Ease of Use	✓	✓
Lead to recommendations, solutions, or policy	✓	✓
Can become (are planned as) part of a "legal" record	✓	Seldom
Are often the basis for betting company's and your future	Y/Y	N/Y

FIGURE 9.1 *Characteristics of effective business and academic reports.*

 **USING THE WRITING AND EDITING PROCESS WITH REPORTS**

Using the writing and editing process (see Chapter 3) can help you and your team create effective reports and understand where the process steps come into play when you are addressing specific report characteristics.

Step 1: Prewriting

Prewriting helps you clarify your thinking before you start writing. Your drafting and editing will be easier and more effective because prewriting helps you:

- Identify your readers or users
- Determine the goals and requirements to be met
- Identify the sequential subtasks to be completed
- Establish individual responsibilities and identify potential conflicts (e.g., work, family, social)

Your Company's Report Standards

In some companies, report-specific or company-specific style requirements vary from department to department. In other companies, company-specific styles and standards may be poorly defined. When they do exist, they may consist of nothing more than vague instructions and generic templates: "Use two columns on a page and use a table here. That's our style," or "Here, make your report look like this one. The boss liked that report." We recommend developing consistent, clear styles and standards for reports.

Report Characteristics	Address in Process Step
Are Written to Meet Needs of Specific Users/ Decision Makers	**Prewriting+**
Have an executive summary that helps users make decisions	Postwriting
Define problem(s) and recommendation(s) up front	Drafting
Are focused, brief, and accurate	Editing
Are functional (inform, document, evaluate, and/or persuade)	Editing
Identify/Justify Assumptions and Opinions	**Editing**
Avoid unintentional bias and distortions of fact and logic	Editing
Use "Company/Group" Standards for Document Layout/Design	**Prewriting**
Use consistent layout/design to show structure/relationships	Prewriting+
Use fonts, heads, and subheads to facilitate understanding	Editing
Use figures/tables/charts to advance/support key points	Drafting+
Provide needed references, footnotes, and in-text citations	Drafting
Require Coordination and Teamwork	**All**
Improved by discussions/negotiations of content	All
Are prepared under tight deadlines and due dates	All
Are often integrated with other reports (within/across areas)	Prewriting+
Are periodically (quarterly, annually) revised/updated	All
Are presented and discussed/defended in meetings	All
Are Planned and Edited for Ease of Use	**All**
Lead to recommendations, solutions, or policy	All
Can become (are planned as) part of a legal record	All
Are often the basis for betting company's and your future	All

FIGURE 9.2 *The relationship between effective reports and the writing and editing process.*

TABLE 9.1 THE BASIC STRUCTURE OF A PERSUASIVE REPORT OR PROPOSAL

1. *Good reports have clear structures.* A useful general report structure includes:

   ☑ **Executive summary.** A stand-alone document that helps your readers understand information and/or make decisions

   ☑ **Introduction.** A paragraph or two on what's coming, where, and its importance

   ☑ **Conclusion/recommendation.** Up front, so your readers aren't left guessing

   ☑ **Body with clear supporting information** (shorter is better)

   - *Coherently organized.* Use organizational patterns (problem/solution, fiscal periods, time sequences, etc.) that reinforce your objective and meet readers' needs.
   - *Supporting data.* Include the necessary data in your text or append it (preferred).
   - *Figures/tables/graphics.* Use visuals that advance your argument, make key points easy to understand, and have labels and visual cues that make points clear at a glance.
   - *Documented sources.* Include citations to help readers judge and validate information.

   ☑ **Summary.** One or two paragraphs to close the report and reinforce conclusions

   ☑ **Collected references/footnotes.** To help readers locate key information sources

   ☑ **Appendixes.** With secondary information in stand-alone, well-introduced sections

2. *Good reports are easy to use.* After reading an executive summary, a reader should know your goal/objectives, conclusion, results or recommendations, and the report's structure (organization). The body of the report is as short as practical. Extra information is appended.

3. *Good reports use visual cues.* Your visual cues reinforce the logic and structure of the report. Your layout/design make your logic/structure visually clear. To help guide your reader and allow the reader to skim the report quickly, use

   ☑ Consistent fonts

   ☑ Concise, meaningful heads and subheads

   ☑ Page headers or footers (author, title, date, page numbers, and computer file name)

4. *Good reports are well written and edited.* If your readers can't easily understand what you have written, your recommendations will have low credibility. When you edit, first edit for logic/organization, then layout, and last for grammar. Remember that good reports have

   ☑ Executive summaries that help readers make decisions

   ☑ Clear organization (problem/solution, sequence of events, concern/recommendation/next steps)

   ☑ Figures/tables that advance/support your argument and link to your presentation

   ☑ Sufficient information/supporting data so your readers can make unbiased decisions

5. *Good reports are short.* Save yourself, your staff, and your readers time by editing your content so that it meets your readers' needs. If you don't know what your readers need, ask them!

- Establish timeline(s) and decide how to track progress on the project
- Establish document layout and design standards for *all* your group's reports
- Decide how reports are okayed for distribution

For more information on the prewriting step, refer to the discussion of prewriting in Chapter 3.

Gantt and/or PERT Charts

To facilitate prewriting tasks, we have found that it is helpful to use simple Gantt or PERT charts to show the relationships among tasks, people, resources, costs, and timelines, as well as to sequence the substeps of a specific project.

Another tool that can help increase the effectiveness of your prewriting step is to create simple visual sketches or networks of ideas. This will help you visualize and analyze the relationships among your ideas and to best sequence them (Figure 9.3). Some people quickly sketch a flowchart with a few identifying words; others create simple or very complex outlines. Simply list your key points and subordinate ideas using bulleted points. Or, if you want to stress the conceptual relationships among ideas, sketch a relational map (networking, mapping) that uses labeled links among your ideas to show key points and relationships.

There are several advantages to creating these visual sketches during your prewriting step:

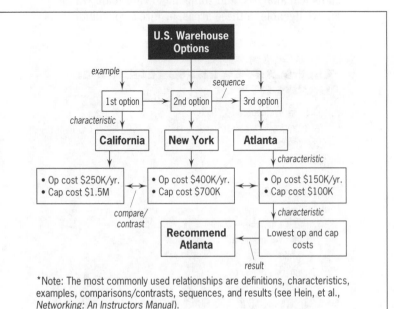

*Note: The most commonly used relationships are definitions, characteristics, examples, comparisons/contrasts, sequences, and results (see Hein, et al., *Networking: An Instructors Manual*).

FIGURE 9.3 *Prewriting technique—visual representations (using labeled relationships* to analyze and link concepts).*

1. They help you see and analyze the interrelationships among your potential topics.
2. They help you take a user's perspective and make certain that your assumptions and "private" knowledge are shared.
3. They help you analyze your assumptions and content, just as your users and critics will be doing.
4. They create a set of reference points so that you don't forget key points in your report or during your presentation(s).

In addition to sketches of concepts in a document, outlines (Table 9.2) and bulleted lists (Table 9.3) can also be effective ways to visualize the actual relationships among ideas.

Step 2: Research and Drafting

After completing your prewriting step, focus on two key ideas as you begin to draft your report:

- Identify your research process and the information or data you need.
- Start writing, shaping your materials to fit your goals, your users, and their requirements.

Research Processes and Techniques

We do not cover research processes or techniques here because of the complexity of the topics. If you haven't been trained in research design, measurement, and statistical analysis, add someone to your team who is knowledgeable in these areas, or hire a consultant. It is

---

TABLE 9.2 PREWRITING TECHNIQUE: AN OUTLINE

Potential U.S. Warehouse Locations
I. Three options
   A. California
   B. NYS
   C. Atlanta
II. Capital and Annual Operating Costs
   A. Capital
      (i) California = unknown
      (ii) NYS = unknown
      (iii) Atlanta = $100M
   B. Annual Operating Costs
      (i) California = $250K
      (ii) NYS = $400K
      (iii) Atlanta = $150K
III. Recommendation: Lowest cost = Atlanta

***TABLE 9.3* PREWRITING TECHNIQUE: A BULLETED LIST**

U.S. Warehouse Options

- California
- NYS
- Atlanta

Capital and Operating Costs

- California (?? & $250K/yr.)
- NYS (?? & $400K/yr.)
- Atlanta ($100M & $150K/yr.)

Recommendation

- Atlanta (lowest cost)

---

critical that you understand the assumptions you are making during your research design, measurement, and analysis tasks. If you don't have good data, and if you don't analyze it correctly, you are likely to write a report that is rejected or, worse, leads to bad decisions.

Drafting Processes and Techniques

After completing any preliminary research and organizing your material, you need to start drafting (writing) your material.

Start writing by reviewing the goals and requirements that you identified in your prewriting step. Start writing on any of your topics or subtopics. Don't force yourself to start at the beginning and write linearly. Start with the topic you know best—one that will flow quickly and easily. Then, build other pieces of your report, using the structure of your outline, flowchart, or visual (relational) map.

Remember, when you are drafting, your goal is to get your ideas down. Worry later about having perfect phrasing and grammar. Don't stop to punctuate your citations or footnotes. Note that you need a figure or a table, but don't stop to create them with painstaking precision. Those are editing tasks, not part of your drafting step. Get your ideas down. Fix them later.

Steps 3-5: Editing

As we explained in Chapter 3, the editing process can be simple or time-consuming depending upon how well you have completed your prewriting and drafting steps.

As you start editing a complex report:

- Refer to the flowchart, outline, or relational map that you sketched during your prewriting step. That diagram will remind you how to sequence your ideas and build the relationships among them.

- Notice where you stumble or have to reread your own report. Make a note at those places to remind yourself to edit that specific material later for grammar or logic.

- Locate places where you can simplify your material by using charts, tables, figures, or diagrams to better show the relationships among complex points. Reducing several paragraphs or pages of text to a useful table, figure, or chart will make your readers very happy.

As you will recall from Chapter 3, we recommend editing for logic, organization/layout, and then grammar. You'll be wasting time later if you don't edit your materials logically and sequentially.

Step 4: Postwriting

The postwriting steps are fundamentally the same for all documents (for more on postwriting, see Chapter 3). For reports, make certain that you validate the adequacy of any figures and tables, the accuracy of your citations and references, and the adequacy of your executive summary.

Remember that most people do not want to write reports. Even fewer want to read them. Executive summaries that allow the report user to make decisions and locate critical sections quickly will greatly increase the effectiveness of your reports. We discuss executive summaries later in this chapter.

STRUCTURING YOUR REPORT SO IT GETS READ

There are several key ideas that will help you improve the reports you write and ensure that they are read. These include avoiding problems and pitfalls, integrating tables and figures, and developing your argument.

Problems and Pitfalls

Notice that the pitfalls and problems identified here can be addressed through the writing and editing process. Common pitfalls and problems[1,2] in all writing, especially in reports, are shown Figures 9.4 and 9.5. Vincent Vinci gives an excellent description of common issues of concerns in his article, "Ten Report Writing Pitfalls."

Another cluster of writing pitfalls are ethical and legal problems. Charles Brusaw, in *The Business Writer's Handbook,* and Joel Bowman and Bernadine Branchaw

Pitfall[1]	Concept	Address in Process Step
Ignoring your audience	Know exactly what your reader(s) want—and deliver it.	Prewriting Drafting Editing (all) Postwriting
Writing to impress	Includes obscure words and unnecessary, trivial detail.	Editing (logic) Editing (grammar)
Having too many aims	A report should not be a barrage of shotgun pellets.	Prewriting Drafting Editing (logic)
Being inconsistent	Use consistent units of measure, technical terms, equations, symbols, hyphenation, punctuation, grammar, etc.	Drafting Editing (layout) Editing (grammar)
Overqualifying	Know the level of detail needed; avoid excessive modifiers.	Prewriting Drafting (research) Editing (logic) Editing (grammar)
Not defining	If you use a common term in an uncommon way, define it.	Drafting Editing (grammar)
Misintroducing	Introductions should give the subject, purpose, scope, and plan.	Drafting Editing (logic)
Dazzling with data	What data is needed to make a decision? Is there too much data? Is data missing?	Prewriting Editing (logic)
Not highlighting	Phrase your key report elements with care, and make them visually striking.	Prewriting Editing (logic) Editing (layout)
Not rewriting	Does each piece of information fulfill the report's objective or increase the reader's understanding? If not, cut it or rewrite it.	Editing (logic) Editing (layout) postwriting

FIGURE 9.4 *Addressing common problems and pitfalls in reports during your writing and editing process.*[1,2]

in *Business Report Writing,*[3] and others cite common legal and ethical problems, as shown in Figure 9.4.

Throughout your writing and editing process, you should anticipate and eliminate potential legal or ethical problems. From individual, company, and work-group perspectives, you need to make a decision during your prewriting process about how to handle legal and ethical concerns. (See Table 9.4.)

Integrating Tables and Figures

One key tool that can help you create more useful reports is the integration of figures, tables, and dia-

Ethical/Legal Problem[2, 3, 4]	Concept	Address in Process Step
Using copyrighted materials	If you need to reprint multiple copies of more than 50 words, or a visual or table, get permission.	Prewriting and Postwriting
Identifying and creating copyrighted materials	Copyright can exist even without a notice; depositing a copy with the Library of Congress helps document a legal record.	Postwriting
Plagiarism	If it isn't yours, acknowledge it with a citation.	Drafting and Editing
Implied contracts	Written materials may constitute an implied contract.	Drafting, Editing, and Postwriting
Defamation (slander, libel)	Defamation, false or unjustified injury to reputation.	Editing
Slander (defamation)	Slander, oral defamation.	Editing
Libel (defamation)	Libel, written defamation.	Editing
Fraud	Deceit to gain advantage . . . misrepresentation of a product . . . hiding the negative.	Editing
Discrimination	See Title 7 of the Civil Rights Act of 1964 (amended).	Prewriting and Editing
Legal records	When you put it in writing, "it" can become part of a legal record during litigation. Sometimes you need to establish a legal record (e.g., protect patents); other times, you are inadvertently documenting and should not be.	Prewriting and Postwriting

FIGURE 9.5 *Common legal and ethical problems in reports.*

grams. Your goal is to reduce the text and make your critical points easier to see and interpret. This requires more than just sticking a graphic into your document. You need to create useful figures, tables, and diagrams— ones that clarify a point, reduce text, and/or advance your argument. You also need to refer to your table or figure in the text, explaining its relevance to the material and providing transitions that link it to the main ideas.

We show how to create useful graphics on our web site (ron-hein.com) as well as in Chapters 4 through 7. When a document uses figures and tables effectively, the concepts in the document are easier to see and interpret.

Developing Your Argument

Another key aspect of writing a good report is to know when you have optimized the organization of your

TABLE 9.4 LITIGATION AND REPORTS: COSTLY ERRORS CAN RESULT WITHOUT A DOCUMENT MANAGEMENT SYSTEM AND DOCUMENT LIFE-CYCLE PROCESS

In the United States, litigation is frequently based on the use of internal company reports. Because reports are frequently key aspects of litigation, we strongly recommend that you evaluate the need for a specific report before you decide to request or write it. We also recommend that you consider what you plan to do if you get information that you don't really want (for example, the fact that your latest product causes cancer).

Legal issues (potential litigation) should be of key concern to managers who request or create business reports—and to those who evaluate whether specific documents are retained or destroyed.

Based on litigation in the 1980s and 1990s (automobile safety, asbestos, and tobacco), reports are subject to subpoena in the United States and various other countries, and they might not be protected by attorney-client privilege or by sending them to another country.

Before you create or request a business report, keep in mind that when you get something you don't want, destroying it can be a criminal act for which you can bear personal responsibility and liability. Before you request a report that has a high probability of containing bad news, decide how you will address the problem—simply denying or destroying the report is not a legal option!

information. Your report needs to present information in a persuasive but not biased manner. Biased reports make the readers feel as though they have not gotten both sides of an argument, which prevents making a reasoned decision. The actual development of persuasive materials and of logical arguments requires extensive discussion, and a number of excellent books provide such information (see Table 9.5).

 USING EXECUTIVE SUMMARIES AND KEEPING REPORTS SHORT

Most business reports are strengthened when they include an executive summary. Executive summaries save you and your readers time and money by focusing your readers' attention and making your arguments more persuasive in the long run.

What Constitutes a Useful Executive Summary?

There are as many definitions of executive summaries as there are problems to be solved. We find that the ideas of Charles Brusaw, et al., on executive summaries in *The Business Writer's Handbook* are a good starting point. Brusaw suggests that your executive summary should:

TABLE 9.5 DEVELOPING AN UNBIASED ARGUMENT IN A REPORT

The actual development of an argument is beyond the scope of this chapter. There are, however, many good sources of information on developing logical arguments in reports and other materials.

Rottenberg, Annette. 1994. *Elements of Argument,* 4th edition. New York: Bedford/St. Martins Press. Part 1: The Structure of Argument; Part II: Writing and Researching Arguments.

Eckhouse, Barry. 1994. *Competitive Writing: Argument & Persuasion in Modern Business.* New York: McGraw-Hill. Good specific, short examples.

Hollihan, Thomas, and Kevin Baaske. 1994. *Arguments and Arguing.* New York: St. Martins Press. Chapter 5: Argumentation and Critical Thinking.

Ramage, John, and John Bean. 1995. *Writing Arguments,* 3rd edition. Needham Heights, MA: Allyn & Bacon (Simon and Schuster). Chapter 3, Writing Arguments.

Wood, Nancy. 1995. *Perspectives on Argument.* Englewood Cliffs, NJ: Prentice-Hall (Simon and Schuster). Chapter 4: A Process for Writing Argument.

Toulmin, Stephen. 1958. *The Uses of Argument.* Cambridge: Cambridge University Press. Theory, see Section III: The layout of arguments.

In addition to applying the basic principles of a good argument as outlined in Tolman and others, remember that in a business setting, the best argument presents information that will *enable* a decision maker to make the best decision. Presenting biased data doesn't facilitate good decision making.

- Consolidate the primary points
- Contain adequate detail to show significance
- Be used to make decisions
- Be written after completing report
- Contain little technical terminology
- Be concise, but use transitions
- Contain no new information (information not in full report)
- Include figures/tables from full report, but does not reference full report's figures/tables
- Contain definitions of all symbols/abbreviations/acronyms
- Inform the reader as to the report's:
    Purpose
    Conclusions
    Scope
    Methods

Recommendations

Findings/Results

The content in an executive summary should be developed to meet the requirements of those reading the report, so they can best understand the issues and make effective decisions.

END POINT

Writing reports is a complex undertaking, which can be simplified when you use the writing and editing process to guide your work. It will help you save time and effort, and it will help you create more effective reports. Write short, concise, well-organized reports that use straightforward organizational patterns. Include a stand-alone executive summary that your readers can use to make decisions. Such reports are well received, useful, and cost-effective to create.

10

Proposals and Requests for Proposals

Proposals and requests for proposals (RFPs) vary widely in scope, ranging from informal conversations to memos to complex documents. This variation makes it important to understand the relationship between proposals and RFPs.

THE RELATIONSHIP BETWEEN PROPOSALS AND RFPs

A good proposal is a mirror image of the requirements established in an RFP. Because of that, the person or team developing the RFP needs to specify carefully what is being requested in the RFP. Skilled bidders supply only what you have requested.

A disorganized or poorly specified set of requirements leads to disorganized proposals or multiple proposals with different organizations, which is an evaluation nightmare.

A Focus on Proposals

In this chapter, we discuss ideas that pertain to both proposals and RFPs, focusing primarily on four topics from the perspective of writing a proposal:

- Formal versus informal documents
- The bidding process
- Writing proposals and RFPs
- Evaluating proposals

We'll link our ideas to the writing and editing steps explained in Chapter 3 so that you can see how to expand the process to include both proposals and RFPs, in addition to creating more useful documents.

For readers who need more technical information on proposals, we strongly recommend *Proposal Preparation*[1] by Rodney Stewart and Ann Stewart (2nd edition or later), published by Wiley-Interscience. The Stewarts' work contains detailed information on proposals and requests for proposals, including content, checklists, timelines, schedules, and samples.

FORMAL VERSUS INFORMAL PROPOSALS

Proposals can vary widely in terms of their complexity and formality—and thus in terms of the cost of creating *and* evaluating them. In order to create a win-win situation (see Fisher and Ury, *Getting to Yes,*[2] Part 1), it is important that the two groups involved in the process (those issuing the proposal and the respondents or bidders) keep each other's perspectives, needs, requirements, and costs in mind.

Simple or Complex Documents

Part of creating a win-win situation is determining whether to request—or create—complex proposals. Requiring bidders to create complex proposals costing tens or hundreds of thousands of dollars can lead to a lose-lose situation in which excellent potential bidders do not bid. On the other hand, requesting overly simplistic proposals can also lead to a lose-lose situation, wherein both groups spend too much time clarifying information. A lose-lose situation can also result when you don't request sufficient information, when you receive inadequate proposals, and when you have to rebid the project.

Table 10.1 illustrates that the range and degree of formality is partially a function of whether proposals are solicited or unsolicited and/or internal or external to a company or group.

Common RFP/Proposal Scenarios

In some scenarios (for example, in the defense industry), RFPs and proposals are extremely complex and are evaluated in great detail. And seemingly minor points of noncompliance can lead to the rejection of proposals that have taken months to develop. In other business settings, proposals and the resulting "contracts" are simply memos within and among busi-

TABLE 10.1 THE DEGREE OF FORMALITY OF SOLICITED/UNSOLICITED, INTERNAL/EXTERNAL PROPOSALS

	Solicited	Unsolicited
Internal	Frequently formal, sometimes informal	Both informal and formal
External	Mostly formal	Both informal and formal

nesses or groups in a company. One of the simplest, yet potentially problematic, scenarios occurs when proposals are requested and developed during informal conversations with little or no documentation. Such undocumented agreements and informal contracts can lead to honest misunderstandings, fraud, litigation, and project failures. If an agreement is important, get it in writing, and iron out problems before a crisis occurs.

A good proposal is actually a mirror image of what is included within an RFP, a request for quote (RFQ), or a request for bid (RFB). If RFPs are poorly written, you will waste time evaluating, rebidding, and negotiating the contract. Putting together a good team, one with the appropriate technical expertise and writing skills, to write critical RFPs and proposals can often save significant time and money.

Unsolicited proposals are a hard sell; they have to be very persuasive to work.

TO BID OR NOT TO BID?

As we have implied, the RFP/proposal process is fundamentally about two groups negotiating. One group issues a request for proposals or an invitation for bids. A second group must decide whether to bid, and, if bidding, how to bid. To an actual bidder, a proposal is—bottom line—an attempt to sell ideas, services, or products successfully.

Caveats for Potential Bidders

As a potential bidder, before you commit your time and resources to developing a proposal, you need to decide if the effort required is justified—and whether you have the ability to deliver, if your proposal were to be accepted. If you decide to bid, your second decision is what to include in your proposal (see the RFP's exact requirements and specifications).

Bidders need to avoid two problematic situations:

● Making a bid for a project that has already been locked up by someone else.

● Having your expertise solicited and used by companies that are merely identifying potential solutions or developing an understanding of costs and problems without actually intending to award contracts. This often occurs when groups are trying to justify the existence of departments or head count.

Successfully identifying these situations is usually a matter of prior experience.

WRITING PROPOSALS AND RFPs

Writing proposals and RFPs should be done in a thoughtful manner, because the language and the specifications set (or not set) within an RFP or an RFB are the first part of a contract with the successful bidder. The second part of that contract is the proposal. The final requirements are specified in precise wording in the letter of authorization and the letter of acceptance (or the revised proposal), which is the third part of the contract/negotiation process.

Write and Edit with Care

Part of writing and editing carefully is to determine the critical items in a project and to specify the requirements for those items precisely. For example, if one and only one specific part is acceptable, specify that part. If, on the other hand, you will accept alternative parts, indicate that fact in your RFP. If you face a $100,000 loss if the project is not completed on time, discuss a penalty clause in the RFP and insert the clause in the letter of acceptance.

Table 10.2 lists critical items that are commonly found in both RFPs and proposals.

What Should You Request in Your RFP?

As is true of most business documents, there is no single correct answer on what to include in an RFP or a proposal—which frustrates managers looking for cookie-cutter solutions.

What you request depends on your project requirements, company policies, the relationship between the bidder and awarder, and legal issues.

TABLE 10.2 WHAT SHOULD BE IN A PROPOSAL OR AN RFP?*

Suggestions for the content of an RFP

1. General instructions to bidders
2. Draft or proposed contract and schedule
3. Statement of the requirements (work)
4. Appendixes

Suggestions for the content of a proposal

1. Technical strategies
   - Your understanding of the problem(s)
   - How you will solve the problem(s)
   - Why your solution will work
   - The nature of your product or solution
   - Your schedule and completion date, including when A starts/ends; when B starts/ends; etc.

2. Management strategies
   How you can carry out the solution
   - Personnel
   - Experience
   - Insight
   - Facilities
   - Internal organization
   - Quality control mechanisms
   - Historical success
   - Outside resources

3. Cost strategies
   - Why the customer can afford it
   - Why the proposal is reasonable/competitive
   - Your direct and indirect benefits
   - Your budget/costs arranged by
     RFP/IFB requirements
     Category (personnel/supplies/equipment/facilities)
     Benefit
     Time period or project phase

*Based on the work of Stewart and Stewart[1]; Penrose, Rasberry, and Myers[3]; and others.

Improving the Logic and Organization of Proposals and RFPs

Using the writing and editing process (Chapter 3) can help you create high-quality RFPs and proposals. Your prewriting step will help you determine what to include and how to organize it. Your editing steps will help ensure that your organizational plan matches your goals. Your postwriting step will help you make certain that you have evaluated the risks and potential gains, as well as whether you have followed any applicable company policies.

Table 10.3 contains a number of tips that can help you avoid problems during the RFP/proposal process.

Building Electronic Templates

To be able to produce proposals in an efficient and timely manner, we suggest building word processing files and templates that contain commonly requested information, such as company financials, company history, key resumes, compliance statements with federal/state/local laws, projects completed, and references. These boilerplates are then easily modified to fit the specific requirements of a project. This approach will save you extensive time and eliminate redundant work efforts.

TABLE 10.3 TIPS FOR WRITING SUCCESSFUL PROPOSALS

Provide What Is Needed in Your Proposal
There are variations or overlaps among different companies' definitions of what makes an adequate proposal. Ask for specific guidelines before you start writing.

Know the Company Letting the Bid
It is important to know various details about the company letting the bid, which might not be specified in the RFP. For example, does the company use a specific supplier for a subcomponent? If so, you might be more successful if you specify that subcomponent and preferred supplier. If there is a compelling reason to use a different subcomponent or supplier, justify it.

When You Win the Bid
Remember, if your proposal is accepted, you will need to live with the proposal and resulting contract. Be certain you can complete the project according to the specified requirements. Litigation is a fact of life.

Executive Summaries
Providing an executive summary of your proposal can expedite the evaluation process by focusing attention on key requirements, how you plan to meet them, and on selling points that make your company a preferred bidder.

EVALUATING PROPOSALS

When evaluating proposals, it is important to follow a systematic process. To enable you to systematically evaluate the various proposals, you need to specify—in your RFP—how bidders should structure (organize) their proposals. Give bidders a specific sequence (organizational plan) for submitting information. When you do so, it will be easier for you to compare multiple proposals, or the content of a specific proposal, quickly and easily.

When you are evaluating a proposal, watch for subtle deviations from your RFP—in both what is stated and what is omitted.

Useful Criteria for Evaluating Proposals

We have found two sets of evaluation criteria that are complementary and extremely useful: those of Penrose, Rasberry, and Myers, in their book *Advanced Business Communication*[3] and those of Stewart and Stewart in *Proposal Writing*. It is important to use *both* sets of criteria because the technical, cost, and management categorization of Penrose provides important insights on how to conceptualize projects, whereas Stewart and Stewart provide critical questions that clarify more specifically what to evaluate.

Penrose stresses three key categories of information that need to be specified in RFPs and used to evaluate proposals:

- *Technical strategies:* Why and how the proposed solution will work.

- *Management strategies:* How the bidder can carry out the solution(s) (their personnel, experience, insight, facilities, internal organization, and quality control mechanisms).

- *Cost strategies:* Why the bid and proposed solution are cost-effective; why proposal is reasonable/competitive.

Similar to the Penrose categories are those used by Stewart and Stewart: (1) *performance suitability* (parallel to technical strategies), (2) *cost factors* (parallel to cost strategies), and (3) *other factors* (parallel to management strategies).

According to Stewart and Stewart, the key questions that you need to consider relative to each area are as follows:

1. *Performance suitability* (technical strategies)
   - Do the bidders completely understand what needs to be done?

- Will the proposed solutions work?
- Will their management strategies work?
    Do they have good internal lines of communication?
    Do they have good relationships with subcontractors?
    Are the work schedules logical and timely?
- Are the qualifications, experience, education, past performance, and quality of key personnel proven?

2. *Cost factors* (cost strategies)
   - Are the cost estimates credible?
   - Have all needed cost factors been included?
   - Are the costs the most probable ones?
   - Historically, are the company's estimates accurate?

3. *Other factors* (management strategies)
   - Financial condition of the company
   - Importance of the project to the company
   - Stability of labor and management
   - Extent of minority and small-business participation
   - Geographic location and distribution of subcontractors and their stability

After you have used these criteria to evaluate the proposals you receive, ask for clarification, in writing, from bidders who show inconsistencies or discrepancies. Such written clarifications will prevent misunderstandings and problems.

END POINT

There are no cookie-cutter answers that provide a single correct way to write an RFP or a proposal. Writing and evaluating proposals and RFPs can be complex projects. If you aren't certain of what your manager or company wants or requires in a proposal or an RFP, take the safe, sane road. *Ask.*

Business Presentations

Is your ability to speak confidently and persuasively to a group an important part of your function as a manager or an executive? Countless surveys of employers and executives over the past two decades have consistently placed oral communication skills among the top five most desired characteristics for a manager.[1] It is no longer possible to advance in a company or graduate program without solid communication ability. Because today's work and academic environments emphasize teams, meetings, and extensive information sharing, oral and written skills are essential.

In Part 3, you'll learn the key process steps and tasks involved in preparing and delivering business presentations:

- Defining your purpose
- Analyzing your audience
- Gathering supporting materials
- Organizing your ideas
- Planning your visual support
- Practicing your delivery
- Preparing for the question-and-answer session
- Evaluating your presentation

In addition, we also discuss how to handle speech anxiety. While this may not be part of the preparation and delivery process for every speaker or every situation, it is a very common concern, and we address it in detail.

In Chapter 2, we described a writing and editing process that can help you write more efficiently and effectively. We advocated using such a process to improve your writing and save you and your company time and money. We advocate that you use a similar, multistep process when preparing your business presentations.

Recognizing the parallels between the writing and editing and presentation processes can be very helpful when you need to create a document and then present it. Mentally linking the two processes should help you recognize and break ineffective habits and establish new ways of preparing more integrated presentations and documents.

Effective presentations will help you:

- Convey information more efficiently and effectively
- Motivate work teams and groups to make faster and better decisions
- Demonstrate proficiency in subject matter to supervisors and clients
- Increase your professional profile and value to the company
- Provide confidence in all areas of communication

By strengthening your skills and improving your understanding of the presentation process, you will be a more efficient and effective speaker in interpersonal, group, and business settings.

Defining Your Purpose

Imagine the following scenario: When you arrive at work, your manager mentions that you need to be in Chicago on the 15th for an important meeting. You note the meeting on your calendar and go on to other business. On the morning of the 15th, you get in your car and drive to the airport, hoping to find a flight to Chicago. You're lucky! You find one. When you arrive in Chicago, you go to the rental car counter, hoping a car will be available. You're lucky! You find one. When you get in the car, you drive aimlessly around the city, looking for your meeting. You're lucky! You see your manager walking into a hotel and you find the meeting.

Sound pretty implausible? It is, but many executives use a similar approach when they "plan" a presentation or a report. They make a note of it, and when the time comes, they plunge right in without planning ahead, without a good idea of where they are going, what they need to accomplish, or how they are going to accomplish it. From a process perspective, they are ignoring a key preparation step of the presentation process. The first step is to define your purpose. (This also applies to writing documents. See Chapter 2 for the prewriting step in writing and editing.)

In order to get to where you want to go, it helps to plan your itinerary, make appropriate reservations, and get directions. Moreover, if you're going to a meeting in Chicago, wouldn't it be nice to know the purpose of the meeting, why you were invited, and your role? Similarly, when you need to write a document or make a presentation, it's best to consider where you want to go rather than just plunging right in.

Because you can't rely on luck, in this chapter we discuss the following three key ideas related to planning business communication:

- Defining your general purpose
- Defining your specific purpose
- Defining your desired results

DEFINING YOUR GENERAL PURPOSE

People in business communicate to fulfill a basic need—typically to inform or persuade. It is important to know what you're trying to accomplish: Does your audience want to be informed, persuaded, or both? Do they want objective information? Do they want to know all the pros and the cons? Do they prefer a subjective evaluation of a problem? When you know your audience's expectations and requirements, you can better define your purpose and organize your ideas.

When you're presenting or writing to inform (for example, conveying the results of a market research study), you goal should be to provide information in the most objective way possible. The presenter (or writer) should present facts and use verifiable data.

In a persuasive presentation, on the other hand, your goal is to support a particular viewpoint for your audience. Your goal is to present those facts and ideas that build support for your appeal. For example, in a persuasive proposal designed to increase your sales force, you might include sales figures, as well as workload and sales call information that support your recommendation.

Your general purpose will be your initial guide as you plan your presentation. Knowing whether you'll be informing or persuading your audience will help you decide if your purpose is primarily to *teach* (to impart knowledge and facts) or to *guide* (to interpret the facts and present alternatives). Next, we will show how your general purpose may also guide your selection of patterns of organization for your writing and speaking.

DETERMINING YOUR SPECIFIC PURPOSE

After you've determined whether your writing or presentation is to be informative or persuasive, you need to better define your purpose by writing a specific, straightforward statement of purpose. This statement of purpose, or basic thesis sentence, will focus your efforts as you zero in on what you are trying to do in your presentation or document. In a document, this sentence should help your readers understand what you are trying to accomplish. In a presentation, it should perform the same function, and it should also stand out: If we asked your audience to hit a buzzer when they heard the thesis, all the buzzers should ring at the same time.

Some people use very blunt statements: "The purpose of this memo is . . ." or "The purpose of my speech is . . ." Less obvious examples might be phrased as follows:

- "I intend to demonstrate why our no-load mutual fund is the best place for your investment dollars."

- "Our market research shows that the population of our target country is getting younger, and in this presentation we will explore ways to attract this younger audience to our product."

- "This afternoon we will describe three key ways in which the new software can streamline our billing processes."

 DEFINING YOUR DESIRED RESULTS

You will find it helpful to define the results you expect to see. This will make you further clarify and focus your message. Typically, you do not state your operational definition to your audience. You use it to help plan your message and evaluate the response, or lack of response, that you receive.

Here are some examples of how you might phrase the desired results of your presentation:

- "After this presentation, 50 percent of the audience will invest in our mutual fund."

- "After this presentation, a majority of managers will vote in favor of the proposal to add staff to the marketing division."

- "This report will clarify the goals of the assessment team, and as a result, every member will be able to participate fully in the next planning session."

END POINT

For a successful presentation or document, you cannot rely on luck. You need to define your general purpose, your specific purpose, and the results you want to achieve.

Business executives may encounter situations that call for special-occasion speeches. These include introductions, tributes, award presentations and acceptances, and eulogies. Guidelines for these special presentations are discussed in Appendix B.

CHAPTER 12

Analyzing Your Audience

We once attended a conference where the keynote speaker was a famous network journalist. His speech was to be the highlight of the convention, and, at the time of the address, over 3,000 people packed the hall. Some were college professors teaching in communication programs; some were professionals working in business or industry.

The speaker began with a rather lengthy, humorous story about airline travel. It did not relate to the eventual subject of his keynote address, but it told us how difficult it had been for him to get to the conference. After this story, the entire keynote speech became his personal analysis of the most prominent figures in the next presidential election. The speech was interesting, and it was humorous, but as we left the auditorium, many of us remarked that we would give the speech a C– or D+ at best.

Why had the speaker failed? His audience analysis had been inadequate or nonexistent. Here he was, a respected journalist speaking to thousands of people responsible for training the next generation of journalists, and he blew it. He didn't take advantage of the opportunity to offer us his perspective on the field or, of more value, advice and guidance we could take back to our classrooms.

Our experience in this situation is not unique. Analyzing the audience is often an overlooked step in preparing business documents and presentations. Successful public speakers (and comedians!) automatically gear their material to their audiences. And just because you aren't performing at the Hollywood Bowl or delivering a keynote address to thousands of admirers doesn't mean you can skip this step. In fact, for businesspeople who frequently communicate with small groups of 5 to 15 people, a thorough audience analysis can be a key to success.

Within both the writing and the presentation processes, your audience analysis is a key preparation step that will help you clarify your goals and objectives.

Most books on public speaking describe audience analysis in terms of demographics—how many males versus females in a workgroup, ages, cultural background, and so forth. We don't find the demographic approach to be very helpful in the small group settings that are common in business. We suggest that you approach audience analysis by answering seven simple but key questions and keeping those answers in mind as you prepare your document or presentation.

WHO WILL BE IN MY AUDIENCE?

The first thing you want to know is who will be at the meeting. Who will be reading the document? What is my relationship to and history with this group of people? Are they peers, supervisors, or subordinates? What do I know about them from our past meetings together? To the extent that you know the people and something about the way they work and think, you can predict their responses to your message and plan your appeal accordingly. For example, you know that one person in your workgroup always objects to new proposals with the argument: "We've always done it this way. Why change?" Knowing the nature of the objections that will arise will enable you to be prepared with a line-by-line comparison of how the new procedure will be superior to the old procedure.

WHAT DOES THE AUDIENCE KNOW ABOUT ME?

An essential concept for a business executive is the idea of credibility. (See Table 12.1.) Do people believe you when you speak? Are they confident that you know what you're talking about?

If you are totally unknown to your audience, it will be helpful for them to have some background information about you—knowing your level of expertise on the topic can lend credence to what you have to say. You can provide this information or, preferably, someone the audience respects might introduce you. Even though boasting is not considered polite in our culture, you should not be modest about your credentials if it helps improve the strength of your message.

TABLE 12.1 SPEAKER CREDIBILITY

Aristotle called it *ethos*. We call it *speaker image* or *credibility*. (Even the ancient Greeks were concerned about a speaker's credibility!) While many have written on the subject of establishing credibility, we have narrowed the concept to three main components.

1. **Knowledge of the topic.** The speaker must be genuinely knowledge-able about the topic under discussion. The audience must perceive that the speaker knows his or her subject matter and is truly an expert. Barring national recognition, you can boost your credibility by using highly credible sources and disclosing those sources to your audience.

2. **Trustworthiness.** The speaker must be perceived as trustworthy by the audience. Generally, audiences seem to trust a speaker unless they are given a reason not to. Credibility is destroyed when the speaker is caught in a lie and, once damaged, is almost impossible to rebuild. (Remember Richard Nixon? Reverend Jim Bakker? Linda Tripp?) Speakers may also be rated low on trustworthiness if they make wild, unsubstantiated claims or are unable to support their points in the question-and-answer session.

3. **Charisma.** A speaker is perceived as more credible to the extent that he or she is dynamic and personable. Good public speaking skills are important; an appropriate appearance and an outgoing and likable personality are also part of the mix.

Experts generally weight these three components of credibility as follows: knowledge, 60 percent; trustworthiness, 30 percent; and charisma, 10 percent. (See Figure 12.1.) However, in the real world, it doesn't always work that way. For example, although leaders of infamous cults (e.g., David Koresh in Waco, Texas, and Jim Jones of Jonestown) can be considered charismatic, if their behavior leads to the untimely deaths of their followers, they could hardly be considered trustworthy. Similarly, politicians who aren't skillful communicators are at a distinct disadvantage in this television age. In the 1984 presidential debates, Ronald Reagan outshone challenger Walter Mondale in spite of Mondale's better grasp of facts and issues. Reagan's dynamic personality overshadowed his challenger's best intellectual efforts.

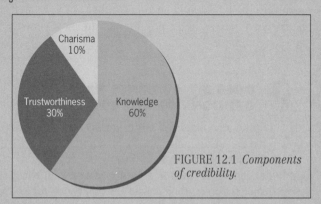

FIGURE 12.1 *Components of credibility.*

So what is the lesson for business speakers who want to earn a reputation for high credibility? First, know your subject matter. Second, do not do anything to make your audience question your trustworthiness. And third, practice your public speaking skills to improve your presentations.

An issue that some of our business students face has been known as the "Y&I factor"—young and inexperienced. If you are younger than your business associates, you may have to work harder to establish your credentials, especially early in your business relationships. In addition to focusing on your own expertise on a particular topic, you may wish to focus on some of the suggestions we offer in Chapter 13 (gathering supporting materials).

WHAT DOES MY AUDIENCE KNOW ABOUT THE TOPIC?

One of the most important factors that will guide a speaker or writer is the level of expertise of the audience. This is a significant factor as you prepare your message, because you should gear your information and appeal to the level of your audience's understanding. For example, typically, a highly technical R&D project would need to be put into layman's terms for a financial group that is deciding whether to support the project. However, that same R&D group would probably present its findings at a much higher technical level at a scientific conference.

A frequent consideration for business executives is the use of jargon in documents and presentations. You need to know your audience's knowledge of the topic in order to know how much jargon you can use. If your message is aimed at too high a level, you run the risk of losing your audience. If your message is aimed too low, they will be insulted and bored, and they will tune you out.

Speakers frequently ask what to do if it's a mixed audience, with varying levels of expertise on the topic. Generally, the talk should be aimed either at the level of the decision makers in the group, or at the most common denominator.

DOES MY AUDIENCE HAVE ANY OPINIONS ON THE TOPIC?

It is a definite advantage for a speaker or writer to know if his or her audience has formed an opinion on the topic under discussion and, if so, whether that opinion is firm or flexible. In a persuasive appeal, writers and speakers plan their messages differently for supportive, hostile, or apathetic audiences. The pattern of organization, the types of supporting materials, and the nature of the appeal all vary, depending on the audience's predisposition toward the topic. Clearly, if you know that most of your listeners—and especially the decision makers—support your ideas, you will have an easier task than if you know that they will be antagonistic. But perhaps the most frustrating situation is one in which the audience just doesn't care about the topic or the message. Then you really have your work cut out for you.

WHAT MOTIVATES MY AUDIENCE?

Motivation underpins our behavior, so it's important for the author of a document or the speaker in a presentation to know what factors might persuade the audience to accept a message. While the list of motivators could be quite long in theory, in the business world, much of the motivation comes down to the bottom line. Does this proposal help your company save money or to make money? Can this new initiative allow employees to use their time more efficiently?

This is not to say that the corporate world is motivated only by greed and profits. However, you need to consider what factors are important to your listeners and incorporate them into your message. Only then can you motivate your audience to pay attention and, hopefully, to accept your message.

WHAT DOES MY AUDIENCE NEED OR WANT TO KNOW?

Another important factor in your audience analysis is understanding what your audience needs to know and/or wants to know. Do your logistics people want to know about what the manufacturing people are doing? They do if they're interested in supply chains, but they might be more immediately interested in other factors. Tailor your speech to what they want to know.

WHAT DO I WANT MY AUDIENCE TO DO AS A RESULT OF OUR INTERACTIONS?

This often comes down to knowing what you (or your managers) want to accomplish as a result of your presentation. Your audience should leave with a clear understanding of what they need to do and what you are planning to do.

RELY ON SITUATIONAL ANALYSIS

Audience analysis should include situational analysis—for both presentations and documents. Variables you may wish to include are:

- Recent developments in the business environment (e.g., rumors of acquisition by a larger company)
- Recent developments within the immediate work-group (e.g., a new reporting line through a financial group)
- Workgroup stress due to a deadline for a major project
- Workgroup satisfaction (or dissatisfaction) due to success (or failure) of a recent project
- Factors involved in the physical work environment, which can even involve conditions in the presentation room (too cold or too warm can distract people from your message)

END POINT

Analyzing your audience is a crucial step in preparing your presentation. It often pays to find out ahead of time what people really think about your proposal or what motivates them toward achieving a particular goal. You may need to take the time to talk to coworkers in order to gain the information you need. However, you will find that the time and effort you expend will help produce the desired response to your message.

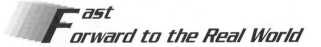

Fast **F**orward to the Real World

Audience Involvement in Presentations

Eric W. Skopec

As Regional Director for Business and Management at Learning Tree University, I have the opportunity to practice techniques of audience involvement on a regular basis. I have learned, practiced, and refined these specific techniques over my years as a college professor, consultant, and administrator, and believe they can work for any speaker in any situation.

Audience Background

Several hundred people attend open houses at Learning Tree University every term. These public sessions are conducted by program directors with the assistance of faculty and other staff. Attendance at each ranges from 12 to over 70, with the average being around 25. Sampling indicates that attendees have a variety of educational backgrounds: About a quarter hold advanced degrees, half have completed undergraduate degrees, and the remainder have a high school education.

In addition, people have a variety of reasons for attending open houses. Most come because they want to make sure they will feel comfortable in the classroom environment. Others attend to get answers to personal questions or to gather information about career opportunities. A few are comparing our programs with those of competitors; a handful want to meet instructors of courses in which they are already enrolled; and a scattering come to provide "moral support" for friends and relatives considering enrollment. The diversity of backgrounds and motives presents a significant challenge for speakers. Adapting to the varying backgrounds and interests is an "on the fly" activity because speakers need to represent the University in an appropriate manner while covering a variety of topics, responding to individual questions, and providing career counseling.

Techniques of Audience Involvement

To cope with the challenges described above, I use a speaking style designed to promote high levels of audience involvement. Here are some of the techniques I find particularly valuable.

Always arrive at least 40 minutes early. I do this to make sure that facilities are ready and to meet my audience one-on-one as they arrive. I will often engage early arrivals in an extended conversation by introducing myself, explaining my role, and finding out what they want to get out of the

(Continued)

(Continued)

open house. As more people arrive, I introduce them to the folks who are already there and convert the audience into an extended conversational group. By the time I begin speaking, I have considerable information about the audience, and they feel comfortable with one another.

Always begin the formal presentation on time. This way I avoid aggravating those who have made the effort to arrive on time. However, I like to postpone discussion of specific programs until stragglers have arrived, so I typically begin by discussing changes in our economy and the need for professionals to continuously reeducate themselves. The material is interesting in and of itself, and it also sets the stage for discussion of specific courses and programs.

While speaking, make it a point to refer to individual members of the audience who posed questions before the session began. I often toss technical questions to faculty members. This ensures that participants get complete and accurate information, and it helps to involve the faculty as well. When I begin discussing classes and certificate programs, I use what I've learned about my audience to address their individual concerns. Whenever possible, I preface statements by acknowledging one or more members of the audience. It sounds something like this: "Before we began, John asked if . . ." or "Mary, here's the material you were asking about . . ." This tactic helps to anchor what I say in specific audience concerns, and invites John, Mary, and other audience members to chime in with additional questions.

Keep the presentation moving. Audiences have an attention span of under an hour, and I generally try to complete my remarks in 40 minutes. In general, I am prepared to speak for 25 minutes, because responses to audience questions occupy the additional 15 minutes.

Avoiding Debates

Occasionally, someone in the audience will appear to argue or disagree with something I've said. To avoid creating the impression of a debate, I use a series of tactics that help to turn objections into opportunities. The first step is to make sure the audience and I fully understand the question. Argumentative tones usually disappear when a person rephrases their question and I can frame my answer while they're speaking. If I have specific information which is relevant, my answer takes the form of a salesperson's response: "I know just what you mean. I felt that way myself until I learned that . . ." I can also turn the question over to a faculty member, and other members of the audience are often anxious to answer on my behalf. After all, it's difficult to attack someone who has gone to the trouble of making you feel at home.

Advantages of Audience Involvement

These techniques work well in most situations, and I use them deliberately because I know high levels of audience involvement help me talk more

(Continued)

(Continued)

intelligently to people with diverse interests and backgrounds. There are also two other advantages:

1. *Audience involvement helps to get hidden agendas out into the open.* Audience members typically have specific concerns and will be lost quickly if a speaker doesn't respond directly. By involving my audience throughout a presentation, I find out what their issues are and can make sure to address them.

2. *Involvement is a key to persuasion and contributes to high levels of enrollment.* Whereas other speakers in similar roles are pleased when 20 or 30 percent of the people present at an open house enroll, it is common for more than three-quarters of my attendees to enroll.

While my situation may sound like a unique one to many, the principles of audience involvement work in almost any type of business presentation. I find them particularly effective in sales and other persuasive presentations for making a group receptive to my message before I even "ask for the sale."

Eric W. Skopec, Ph.D., is the Regional Director for Business and Management at Learning Tree University in Los Angeles, California. He formerly served as a Partner for Strategic Visions Consulting Groups and Director of Executive Education Programs for the Graduate School of Business Administration at the University of Southern California. He is the author of nine books, including How to Use Team Building to Foster Innovation Throughout your Organization *and* The Practical Executive and Team Building.

Gathering Supporting Materials

The extent to which you can justify your point, support your position, and make your case often determines the success of your presentation. The successful communicator knows that strong support for ideas can often determine the audience's perception of your credibility on the topic as well as the outcomes after the speech is over.

Many managers and executives probably haven't given much thought to the idea of formal supporting materials, such as you would use for a college research paper, because data and information are so readily available within their work environment. People working in business often use materials, such as financial reports, market research, and projections, to construct their written documents and presentations. The topic is set, the data is available, and they use that data as they plan the message. What they lose sight of is how important it is to translate data and projections into information the audience can use. Part of gathering supporting materials involves building a unique point of view that adds new meaning to what was previously thought of as mere data. (See Table 13.1.)

We will cover two major topics relating to supporting your ideas. First, we examine the types of supporting materials that are available to use in documents and presentations. Second, we offer guidelines for the effective use of supporting documentation.

TABLE 13.1 HOW MUCH SUPPORTING MATERIAL?

Gathering supporting material is an important task in both the prewriting step and in the preparation step of the presentation process. Experts recommend that you gather three times as much material as you need. Doing so enables you to:

- Choose only the best evidence to help you make your case
- Have extra background information in the question-and-answer session
- Feel more confident with a higher level of knowledge on the topic
- Relieve any speech anxiety you may experience

TYPES OF SUPPORTING MATERIALS

There are five types of commonly used supporting materials:

- Statistics
- Definitions
- Examples
- Comparisons and contrasts
- Testimony and quotations

Statistics

Numbers and data are most likely going to be an integral part of any business presentation. Unfortunately, many managers think that if they have some statistical data, they automatically have a presentation. One Eastman Kodak executive told us he spent *six hours* in a meeting looking at charts and graphs.

Merely showing data is not the same thing as delivering a presentation. You should be judicious in selecting the data you wish to use. If you present only those numbers that are crucial to the central idea of your message, they will stand out as persuasive and will increase the impact of your verbal message. Additionally, you should be sure that any data you present is well designed so the message is instantly clear (see Chapter 5 on layout and design).

Definitions

How you use definitions in your presentation will depend on your audience analysis. There are two types of definitions: literal and stipulated. You may use a *literal definition* if you are using jargon or technical language with which your audience may not be familiar. For example, novice investors may not know the difference between a load and a no-load mutual fund. Alternatively, you might use a *stipulated definition* when the usage in a particular field may differ from the norm—for example, Stephen Covey uses the term *ecological balance* to describe an organizational environment. This stipulated definition varies significantly from the way biologists might describe a balanced ecology.

Examples

The use of examples is an excellent technique for showing the application of your presentation material to your audience. Examples can make your presentation come alive and break up the monotony of a long presentation. They may be real or hypothetical. *Real examples* have the advantage of being verifiable. Your audience knows that it happened and that your information has validity.

At the same time, *hypothetical examples* can be equally helpful for the speaker. They can be used to draw the audience into the material and to make the presentation really hit home. This can be especially true if you use audience members for your examples. A speaker might say something like this: "Let's say Joe needs to verify his data. He could contact anyone in Mary's department and they would have the information if they were hooked up to the network." This hypothetical example draws both Joe and Mary into the presentation (it's difficult to let your mind wander when the speaker is talking about you!), and it also demonstrates how the information can be applied to this particular workgroup.

If the situation is somewhat informal, a speaker may also use the classroom teacher's technique of asking an audience member to provide an example. But don't try this unless you are confident you have a responsive group!

Contrasts and Comparisons

This type of supporting material works well when a speaker is explaining something new to an audience. Comparing new information to something familiar makes it easier to understand. You might explain how to operate a VCR by comparing its control buttons to those on an audiocassette recorder. Or you could describe an updated version of PowerPoint by describing the ways in which it is similar to the earlier version and the ways in which it is different.

Testimony and Quotes

Even if you are an expert in your field, it is nice to have the support of others who agree with your position. These experts could be as prominent as Federal Reserve Board members or Harvard economists, or they may be supervisors and colleagues who have provided you with information. Either way, you should acknowledge anyone who has contributed to your presentation. You may simply say, "Steve's department provided these figures on sales revenue." Not only does that give the credit where it is due, but (assuming Steve is highly regarded by his colleagues) it can improve your own credibility on the topic.

GUIDELINES FOR USING SUPPORTING MATERIALS

The following guidelines pertain to the accuracy of your materials, giving credit for ideas and sources, using a variety of materials, and being creative.

Be sure your supporting material is accurate. People in your audience who are be familiar with your topic will find any errors in data, procedure, process, or sources. Check your document and presentation visuals for typos and accurate figures. Simply spell checking is not enough. You should proofread your material and ask a colleague to proof it also.

Give credit where it is due. You help your own credibility as a speaker and avoid the appearance of plagiarism when you cite your sources for information. Whether your source is a Stanford research study or a colleague who supplied figures on inventory, letting your audience know where you got your material will go a long way toward improving the impact of your message. In a formal report, you might do this by using footnotes. In a presentation, often a passing mention will suffice ("According to figures from the government's General Accounting Office . . ."). If the information is important and has been supplied by a team member or a member of another group who made a special effort to obtain it for you, make certain that you clearly acknowledge your source. It is the right thing to do, and it will help build teamwork and your image as a team player.

If you do not give a source (a publication or data set) during your presentation, make sure you know where you got the information in case the issue comes up in the question-and-answer session.

Try to use variety in your supporting materials. As we mentioned earlier, many managers tend to rely too much on graphs and data and not enough on other aspects of organization and support. Your listeners will be more responsive and will find it easier to pay attention if you use a variety of ways to support your ideas. For example, after you have shown a numerical table or graph, give an example of what it might mean: "We plan to have every high school student in Los Angeles familiar with our new software package by the year 2000." Or you might make a comparison with a familiar reference: "Finding this information was a task even Sherlock Holmes would find daunting."

Don't be afraid to try some creativity in your supporting materials. Think of ways that you can make the facts, data, and ideas come alive for your audience. Find an example that supports your point—or make one up yourself. Find experts who agree with your viewpoint and quote them directly or in paraphrase.

We recently saw the creative use of supporting materials by the chairperson of a Parents Athletic Advisory Committee, who went before the local board of education to discuss the need for a new pool for the district. First, the presenter used color photographs of deteriorating masonry and corroded pipes to dramatize the problems with the old pool. Second, rather than simply saying, "The pool is used constantly during the day," the speaker used a slide to present a detailed list of the school and community groups using the pool from 6:30 A.M. through 9:30 P.M. This simple tactic served to show board members the faces of real people who are affected by their decisions.

END POINT

While you may not generally think about supporting materials when planning your presentations, making this a routine part of your preparation will increase your credibility with your audience and your confidence with your material. Gathering your material before you begin drafting your ideas or outlining your talking points is a key part of your presentation process, as well as the prewriting process. Collecting thorough documentation enables you to select the best and most significant material for your presentation, which in turn will increase your credibility as a presenter and reduce your anxiety.

Once you have the supporting materials you need for the presentation, you are ready to begin organizing your main ideas. You have completed the first three steps of the prepresentation process: defining your purpose, analyzing your audience, and gathering your support. In the next chapter, we'll discuss organizing your ideas.

14

Organizing Your Ideas

A good presentation is like a good story: It has a beginning, a middle, and an end—in that order! In material on writing and editing in Chapter 3, we imparted the "Army approach" to giving messages:

- Tell them what you're going to tell them.
- Tell them.
- Tell them what you've told them.

These straightforward statements also describe a sound, basic approach for organizing presentations.

In this chapter on organization, we'll discuss the introduction, body, and conclusion of a presentation, and we'll make the case for using a thesis or purpose statement.

We've organized the material in this chapter in the order in which you will actually deliver the presentation, but these individual parts—introduction, body, conclusion—do not necessarily need to be prepared in that order.

If you have just thought of a great idea for an introduction or a great quote that will work well in the conclusion, set it aside for later. You should begin by writing your thesis or purpose statement. Next, you should organize your main ideas. After you have done the major work on these two sections, you will have a clearer idea of the most appropriate way to introduce and conclude your presentation.

KEY CONCEPT INTRODUCTIONS

Introductions tell your audience, very clearly and concisely, what you are going to tell them. This is a crucial point in your presentation because you are giving your listeners a template, an organizational structure, that they can use to anticipate your points and, most important, to see how your ideas pertain to them.

This is where you help them anticipate the so-what factor that lurks in the minds of most people who sit down to listen to a presentation. You can be more effective when you answer their most basic questions: "Why am I sitting here, and what do I need to do after we leave?"

When novice public speakers are confronted with introducing a presentation, they often think of beginning with a joke. While jokes may be appropriate in some settings, we recommend you begin by thinking about *the purpose of your introduction.*

A good introduction should accomplish four key tasks:

1. *Inform the audience why it is there.* To improve the likelihood that you will be successful, you need to help people understand why they've come to hear you, what they are going to hear, and what they are expected to accomplish after they leave.

2. *Capture the audience's attention.* People don't pay attention well. There may be distractions in the room. People may be thinking about their own presentations or perhaps daydreaming about lunch. You need to do something to get your audience to focus on you. However, if you begin with your all-important thesis/purpose statement, those who are not paying attention will miss the reason for the presentation.

3. *Focus on the topic.* In the introduction, you should begin to get people thinking about the topic you will be discussing, and you should appropriately reflect the tone of the topic. That is why an irrelevant anecdote or humor simply for humor's sake doesn't work.

4. *Establish your own credibility.* The audience will be making a snap judgment about your abilities as a speaker and your expertise on the topic. Their impressions will probably be formed in the first 30 seconds . . . or less.

 First Impressions

You need to make a good first impression with your content and delivery. If your audience is unfamiliar with your credentials, you should introduce yourself and your background. This is no time for undue modesty: Be candid about your experience and expertise. If an audience is unfamiliar with your background, you must show them why they should listen to you and pay attention to your message.

 Under no circumstances should you do anything to hurt your credibility. For example, do not insult the audience, even as a joke. While this may work for stand-up comedians in a comedy club, it rarely helps your image in a business presentation. Other common errors occur when people jest about their credentials or the fact that they don't know why they were chosen to present. Making such statements establishes a barrier that you will then need to overcome.

KEY CONCEPT Beginning a Presentation

Among many choices, we offer five excellent ways to begin a presentation:

1. *Begin with humor.* If your opening comment is light, sensitive to your audience, and relates to the topic, by all means, use humor. Audiences like to laugh; they can let off a little energy after being forced to sit in one place for a while.

   Humor may also serve to bond you with the audience. Self-deprecating humor on the part of the speaker works particularly well because few can take offense if you poke fun at yourself. (For more guidelines on using humor, see "Fast Forward to the Real World: The Role of Humor in Business Presentations" at the end of this chapter.)

2. *Begin with a question.* This is often an effective way to involve audience members in your presentation. This might be an actual question to which you would like a response ("How many of you have used catalog shopping in the last 30 days?"), or it might be a rhetorical question ("Have you ever thought of what it might be like to navigate the halls of this building in a wheelchair?"). Questions can be extremely useful as conceptual organizers if you phrase them to help your listeners anticipate where your presentation is going.

 If you use the question technique, be sure to clarify whether you want a response. The audience generally likes to cooperate, but no one wants to be the first to make a mistake. And be careful of using this technique for potentially sensitive issues ("By a show of hands, how many of you have ever answered a personal ad in a newspaper?").

3. *Begin with a narrative (or an extended example).* You can tell a story that relates to your topic and illustrates the purpose of your presentation. Journalists doing

feature stories often use this technique. Instead of merely describing health care legislation, for example, a reporter might find a family that cannot afford health insurance and open with a profile of that family.

4. *Begin with a startling statement to get attention.* "According to the Port Hope Police Department, you have a 25 percent chance of being the victim of a violent crime in this city. That means that out of the 20 people in this room, 5 of us could be victimized in the next 12 months." If you dramatize, make certain that your figures are accurate.

5. *Use a concrete example.* Other techniques, including real-life examples of a key point, can also be used as an engaging opener. For example, in one of our undergraduate classes, a student discussing teen pregnancy brought in her three-year-old daughter. Another speaker began a presentation on violence in the movies by showing videotaped clips from films. Each was a very effective, attention-grabbing start.

KEY CONCEPT   CREATING THE THESIS STATEMENT

It would be nice to think that a good introduction will get your audience to listen intently to your presentation. But, because people are generally poor listeners, we recommend adding a fourth component to our three-part organizational pie. In addition to the introduction, body, and conclusion, we recommend using a thesis statement.

Many people think of the thesis, or purpose statement, as part of the introduction, and it does, indeed, come at the end of your introduction. However, we are discussing it separately here in order to stress its importance in successfully setting the agenda of your presentation from the outset. (See Table 14.1.)

In Chapter 11, "Defining Your Purpose," we discussed how to define a thesis statement for your document or presentation. Your thesis should be stated immediately after you introduce your presentation. It not only gives your audience a clear sense of your direction and plan, it also helps them comprehend and retain your message. For longer presentations (those exceeding five minutes), we recommend that you follow your thesis sentence with a preview of your entire presentation. This is also a useful tool if you are doing a presentation with multiple speakers because it allows you to both introduce your team and to identify who will be doing what.

Here's an example of how to preview your entire presentation after giving your thesis statement:

INTRODUCTION   Fire. We are fascinated by fire. We enjoy warming ourselves by a roaring fire in the

TABLE 14.1 THE DEVELOPMENT OF A THESIS SENTENCE

Topic: Using ACME Outplacement Services

General purpose: To inform	General purpose: To persuade
Specific purpose: To let the audience know what services are available to them	Specific purpose: To convince the audience that they should contract with our firm for downsized employees
Thesis sentence: *Today we will review the services offered by our office.*	Thesis sentence: *Today you'll understand why we're the first choice among outplacement firms to service your needs.*

winter, and yet fire can be terrifying when it is out of control. As a member of the Fire Safety Team for XYZ Company, I've had training in many aspects of fire safety.

THESIS   Today, I would like to discuss fire safety in the workplace and offer some tips you may use at home as well.

PREVIEW   I plan to discuss three major areas: the kinds of fires we may encounter, what to do if you encounter a fire at work or home, and ways that these fires may be prevented.

In this example, the speaker introduces the topic, clearly lays out a purpose, and then previews the scope of the presentation. (Note that the speaker has also established credibility by giving personal credentials on the topic.) More examples of thesis statements can be found in Table 14.2.

TABLE 14.2 EXAMPLES OF THESIS STATEMENTS

- This afternoon we'll be going over the new procedures for appraising your employees and answering any questions you might have about the changes in the compensation system.

- Today we'll review the suggestions that have been made to deal with the inventory crisis and ask for your input about which one is most likely to solve our problem.

- I'll be showing you just how easy it is to enroll in our Executive MBA program and earn your degree in two years without interrupting your career.

- This merger will bring big changes to our company, and today we'll look at how it will specifically impact each of your departments.

- There are a number of ways to reduce the cost of your health insurance, and this morning we'll review several of the new options being offered.

DEVELOPING THE BODY

To continue our "Army" analogy, the body of the presentation is where you "tell them"—where you impart your content. When you begin to organize the body of your message, you are, in a sense, drafting, just as you would in the writing and editing process. Your goal is to get your main ideas down. You're thinking about logic and structure, just as you do when you're preparing a written document.

To develop the body (the content) of your presentation, your need to focus on two main areas: (1) organizing your ideas for maximum impact and (2) using transitions to link your ideas effectively.

Organizing Your Ideas

The ideas within the body of the speech must be put forth in an organized way. Most of us are familiar with common patterns of organization: chronological, spatial, topical, and so forth. For example, a presentation about budget forecasting will generally proceed in a chronological format.

Indeed, the organizational patterns of most messages are frequently very obvious—after you have been listening for a few minutes. Our goal is to make certain that you don't lose your audience for those first few minutes.

If you have a clear pattern of organization, much of your strategy is set. In the preceding example on fire safety, the speaker makes it easy for the audience to follow the message by previewing how the presentation is organized.

If you do not have a clear pattern of organization, you need to develop one so that the point of your message is clear. Deciding how to organize the body of your presentation sometimes depends on your topic; other times, it depends on your audience. For example, if you are planning a persuasive appeal but your audience has no knowledge of the topic, you'd probably choose to begin in a more informative way. On the other hand, if you're making a presentation to an audience that already knows about the topic, you probably should begin more subjectively, appealing to your best talents of persuasion.

When one speaker we know was presenting a plan for a multilevel marketing company, he found out that few members in the group were familiar with the concept of multilevel marketing. Therefore, he began by teaching the concepts, and only then was he able to pitch his particular product in a way the audience could understand. By finding this out beforehand through careful audience analysis, he was able to avert what could easily have been a disastrous presentation.

The writing and editing information in Part 2, Chapters 3 and 4, is a helpful guide to organizing your ideas and editing for logic and unity. (See "Tech Tools: Outlining with Software.")

OUTLINING WITH SOFTWARE

While many writers and presenters still like to sit down with a pad of paper or note cards to outline their ideas, more and more people are using their computers. Most word processing programs now come with an "outline view" mode that enables you to organize your main points, subheads, and transitions right on the computer screen. These are helpful because they provide you with a structure to follow and a way to keep your ideas organized. However, you must still do the conceptual work of pulling out the main and subordinating points and fitting them into the pattern that matches your presentation.

Many presentation software programs include templates that actually give you an outline for organizing ideas according to the type of presentation you are creating. For example, Microsoft PowerPoint provides "Auto Content Wizards" for such presentations as Motivating a Team, Recommending a Strategy, Reporting Progress, and Introducing a Speaker. Such templates may be helpful to the novice who has little company support in the area of business communication. However, most managers find the templates cumbersome to use and too confining in terms of breadth and depth of content. If you are familiar with your topic area and have a clear purpose and solid audience analysis, you will probably find it more expedient to prepare your own pattern of organization.

While you're organizing the ideas in your presentation, don't forget about the supporting material you have worked so hard to gather. Your data charts, examples, comparisons and contrasts, definitions, and testimony from others can be key variables in making your point. For some presentations, the supporting material will be a main point—for example, figures on turnover and absenteeism might be a main topic for a presentation on improving the quality of work life in an organization. In other circumstances, you may want to place supporting material where it will help buttress a specific point. For example, in explaining a new billing system, you might find it helpful to use contrast and comparison—showing similarities and differences between the old and new systems. This linkage will help your audience follow your message and understand how to use and apply the new system.

KEY CONCEPT **Transitions**

An important yet often overlooked step for your presentation planning involves paying particular attention to the *transitions* that you use to link your ideas together. For audiences, transitions serve as signposts, as guides that help them navigate the points of your message. Transitions are crucial: If you ignore them, your audience can be left floundering, even if you have created a well-organized document or presentation.

Transitions can be as simple as a single word (such as *therefore*) that denotes you are making a concluding statement based on your preceding ideas. Transitions can also be internal summaries: "Now that we've outlined our cost overrun problems, let's look at possible solutions."

Another very effective transition is to number your points: "Today I'd like to describe three key ideas: Number one . . ." With such a quick lead-in statement, you can help your audience anticipate where you're going and guide them to the desired outcome. (See Table 14.3.)

DANGER! You don't want to add your transitions too early in the presentation preparation process. As you edit, you'll no doubt change ideas around. This can happen even during the practice sessions. If you work on transitions too early in the process, you will spend valuable time on a step that will probably be changed later.

KEY CONCEPT **MAKING A CONCLUSION**

A key summary step in delivering your presentation is "telling them what you told them." Once you have gone through the main points of your presentation, you are ready to conclude. You need to accomplish two main tasks with your conclusion:

- Reinforce your topic, purpose, or main points.
- Provide closure or completeness to your presentation.

When you are done, it should be clear to the audience that you are finished speaking and that it is time for the question-and-answer session—or for applause!

To be effective, tailor your conclusion to the audience and reinforce the points that you want them to take away. For most speakers, this involves one or more of the following:

- A summary of the main points of the presentation
- A restatement of the thesis
- An appeal or challenge to the audience

TABLE 14.3 SAMPLE TRANSITIONS

Transitional Words

- and
- but
- therefore
- thus
- moreover
- additionally

Transitional Phrases

- not only . . . but also
- on the one hand . . . on the other hand
- in addition to . . .
- considering the circumstances . . .
- as a result of this . . .
- either/or . . . neither/nor

Transitional Strategies

- numbering points
- lettering points
- internal summaries

We are frequently asked if it is acceptable to say, "In conclusion . . ." in a business presentation. We have a particular bias against this phrase because we have found many speakers use it as a crutch to avoid developing an effective transition to their conclusion.

Worse, one speaker indicated that he used the phrase to get the audience to pay attention for another 20 minutes! Please don't try that idea. When you tell your audience you are going to conclude, then you need to conclude!

Example of a Good Ending

Our earlier example of a fire safety speaker lends itself to showing a well-thought-out transition for concluding:

> *There are few things in life more tragic than being the victim of a fire. Hopefully, I have given you some insights on how you can both avoid becoming the victim of a fire and protect your coworkers or family. Remember, there is no substitute for prevention and preparation: Check the*

batteries in your smoke alarm; have an escape route planned; and leave being a hero to the professionals.

END POINT

Having well-organized thoughts is the key to a great presentation. A clear, logical, and tight presentation can help your listeners comprehend your message and enhance your credibility as a speaker.

When you organize your materials, you will probably find it helpful to return to your thesis statement, your audience analysis, and your supporting materials as you develop your strategy. You may find, for example, that you need more data to support your point or that you need more information on how strongly your audience favors your proposal.

When you are confident of the structure and organization of your presentation, you also will be able to convey your message—and your credibility—clearly and effectively.

Fast
Forward to the Real World

The Role of Humor in Business Presentations

Judythe A. Isserlis, Ed.D.

What is the role of humor in public speaking? In generalizing about the role of humor in public speaking, it is useful to think about the role humor can play in our lives. According to humor expert Harvey Mindess:

- Humor is the social glue that keeps us together.

- Humor can ease tension and create a bond between you and your audience (this is true even for an audience of one other person).

- Humor can help to disarm a hostile audience.

- Humor can serve to focus the attention of your listeners, because when people laugh, they notice the source of the laughter and attend to it.

- Humor can help your listeners to understand and to remember your important ideas, thus creating an opportunity for you to have greater impact than you might have had otherwise.

- Humor that is effectively placed can ultimately be a tool of persuasion.

- Humor is fun for the speaker—either in a conversation, group situation, or in a public speaking situation.

Given all of the potential benefits to using humor in a presentation, why not throw caution to the wind, stock up on the most recent Internet jokes (some of which are as current as the day's news), and use them liberally throughout all of your speaking engagements? Actually, there are quite a few reasons why you should not do this. In order to be able to use humor effectively (and it is a technique that can be used by all of us), it is first necessary to debunk some of the common misconceptions that speakers have about humor in general.

When we discuss humor in presentations, aren't we referring to jokes? First of all, humor and jokes aren't synonymous. Jokes typically have a beginning, a middle, and an end, and rely on a punchline for their effect. A well-placed joke that is pertinent to the topic at hand can be most effective in a speech. Often, however, you'll have difficulty finding these; most jokes have to be tailored to the specifics of your speech.

Humor, on the other hand, can be much more spontaneous and informal, but humor in general, like any specific joke, doesn't exist in a vacuum. Although the idea of humor is universal, the specifics of what a particular audience will find funny depends on the context and the speaker.

For example, during a recent, sold-out appearance by Jerry Seinfeld, the comedian asked a New York audience (without introducing the topic),

(Continued)

(Continued)

"So what about those New York cab drivers and their BO?" The audience roared with laughter and gave Seinfeld a round of applause. This question was certainly not a formal joke with a beginning, a middle, and a punchline ending, but the audience was demonstrably responsive.

The question is, "Why?" First of all, the context certainly encouraged the audience's reaction. Seinfeld is one of the most popular comedians in the country, and he was playing to a sold-out house. He was expected to be funny, and the audience was inclined to laugh. Seinfeld also had the credibility of being a funny, extremely insightful comic who casts light on the daily travails of urban life. His pointed reference to a specific aspect of New York City urban life demonstrated how he identified with his particular audience. This one-liner would not have worked as well anywhere other than in New York. Therefore, it appeared that both Seinfeld's reputation and his identification with his audience were the factors in making an offhand, trivial question (which was not inherently humorous) hilariously funny in his routine for that time, place, and audience.

The question for the business presenter is this: What can a speaker such as yourself—not a famous comic whose reputation precedes him—learn from Seinfeld's humorous one-liner? This is the lesson: *Humor is specific to a particular context, which includes the audience's perception of the speaker, the audience itself, the time, the place, the subject, and the goal of the speaker.* This implies that much successful humor occurs within the speaking situation itself. What this means is that you, the speaker, need to carefully analyze the context in which you are speaking.

Humor can be very effective, even as an offhand comment, as is illustrated in the following example:

> A management consultant was hired by a large corporation to conduct a number of training sessions on internal communications. He began his presentation by making reference to the extensive security checks he (and everyone else entering the building) had experienced. He noted with a smile that the security measures had given him a head start toward his next annual physical exam. The audience smiled. The offhand comment turned out to be an effective way of creating goodwill and rapport. The speaker was able to tap into a unifying experience and incorporate a humorous moment into a presentation. Humor doesn't have to be riotously funny to be effective. No audience expects you to be a comic, but humor comes in many forms.

Can I use humor even if I don't consider myself a funny person? We hope the preceding example gave you the answer. Using *some* humor in a presentation is more a function of the context (an interaction among the speaker, the audience, and the physical environment of the speech) and of the topic itself than it is about your own self-perceived comedic abilities. But of course your own personal style is relevant to the type of humor you might choose. It helps if you've examined your own style:

(Continued)

(Continued)

- Are you sarcastic or witty?
- Do you enjoy one-liners or humorous anecdotes?
- Are you a person who loves to tell a joke and can tell it well?

These are all issues to consider before using humor in a presentation. If you've never enjoyed telling a joke to a small group of friends or business colleagues, it isn't likely that you'll enjoy telling a joke in your next public presentation. The humor you use in a speech, in addition to reflecting the context, will also be a reflection, to some degree, of who you are. It may be, for example, that you find humor in unexpected or incongruous aspects of your own life. These types of observations may be most appropriate to the business topic of your presentation. You can often achieve humor by creating it out of your experiences and your own observations of the world. But, again, you don't have to be hilariously funny to use humor effectively, and you don't have to tell a joke to incorporate humor into a presentation. Your ultimate goal for the presentation is to accomplish your specific purpose. If humor helps, then by all means, consider it.

What are the guidelines for using humor in a speech? If humor is so effective in accomplishing my goal, shouldn't I attempt to use humor as much as possible? As we stated earlier, using humor in your speech may be very useful in accomplishing your objective for the presentation. But there are certainly times to avoid it. Some topics are generally too serious for us to attempt to use humor. If the goal of your presentation is to announce and detail the restructuring and downsizing of your organization, it would appear that the topic itself would dictate a most careful and tactful approach.

In addition to the seriousness of the topic, another consideration is what your use of humor will accomplish. You want the humor in your presentation to be a means to your end—not the end itself. You ultimately want your audience to remember and be instructed by your informative objective, or to change their beliefs, reinforce their beliefs, or take action through your persuasive argument. You don't want the audience to be distracted by your humor. Even in a speech of tribute—for example, a presentation at your colleague's retirement dinner—you need to remember that your goal is to acknowledge and offer appreciation to your colleague rather than being humorous for its own sake (unless, of course, the format for the dinner is a "roast"). Humor should always be the means by which your objective can be met, not the objective itself, and a little humor goes a long way in accomplishing your goal.

Is there any type of humor that should be avoided? It's important to determine what types of humor you should generally avoid in your public speaking, although there can be exceptions. In general, most humor experts agree that you should not use humor that depracates or puts anyone down—with the exception of yourself. This is not to say you should beat yourself up in front of the audience, but it doesn't hurt to laugh a little at

(Continued)

(Continued)

your own expense. (This could backfire, too—you certainly don't want to undermine your credibility for a new audience.) You also should avoid, as a general rule, off-color stories or jokes that might offend any audience member. With the exception of the humor you employ in your introduction (which should be brief and lead gracefully into your topic), your comic moment should be related to your topic. Any humorous analogy or ancedote you use in the body of your speech should be a means of explanation or amplification. Set materials or jokes can be adapted for different audiences by changing the "peg" of the joke (the subject, the character, or the setting); otherwise, set materials that have no direct application for the particular audience should usually be avoided.

Dr. Judythe Isserlis is Chair of the Department of Speech Communication Studies at Iona College in New Rochelle, New York. She has conducted communication training for the American Management Association, Bell Laboratories, and Mobil Oil Company, among others. She has presented research on humor to the International Society for Humor Studies, and has published articles on humor in the Speech Communication Annual *and* New Dimensions in Communication.

Planning Visual Support

A key element in the preparation of any business presentation is the use of visual aids. Often, your decisions regarding visuals happen when you prepare for your presentation and conduct an audience analysis. You'll evaluate who will be in your audience and decide what kinds of information will be most persuasive.

While colorful PowerPoint slides and fancy projection systems have become all the rage in many business settings today, computer-generated visuals may not be appropriate in every situation. Indeed, there are times when you may want less sophisticated visuals— or no visual aids at all.

For example, local health clubs often have their fitness instructors conduct seminars for community groups. For those seminars, the instructors create a stronger visual impact by using themselves as demonstrators and distributing handouts.

In a recent survey in *Presentations* magazine, 96 percent of the respondents agreed that, in general, technology enhances presentations. However, 54 percent also agreed that technology can detract from a presentation.[1]

In Chapter 5, we provided examples of how to improve the layout and design of visuals that you use in written documents. These basic examples are also pertinent to the design of visuals in presentations; however, there are key modifications (for example, font size, color, and complexity) that need to be made. We demonstrate some of these differences by providing before-and-after examples in this chapter to show the characteristics of good visual aids. You'll learn how to plan and improve the visual supports for your presentation.

We cover four primary topics in this chapter:

- Why use visual aids?
- Types of visual aids
- Characteristics of good visual aids
- Guidelines for using visual aids

WHY USE VISUAL AIDS?

KEY CONCEPT

In his early work, *Business and Professional Speaking,* Eric Skopec, now Regional Director for Business and Management at Learning Tree University in Los Angeles, maintains that there are two main reasons to use visual aids: to make ideas memorable and to display complex relationships.[2] As Skopec discusses, it's important to help your audience remember information, and you can do this by giving them more than just an oral presentation. Research on learning supports the idea that stimulating more of our senses (e.g., both seeing and hearing information) improves comprehension and retention.

Eric's second point is equally important—visuals can help explain relationships and ideas that are too complex to understand easily by just listening. For example, it is easier to understand sales forecast figures when you talk about them at the same time you present them graphically.

Beyond Skopec's basic rules, the following are additional reasons to insert visuals into your business presentations:

- They break up the text of a long presentation.
- They help alleviate speech anxiety because you focus the audience's attention on something other than the speaker.
- They demonstrate your skill with newer technologies.
- Your efforts look more professional than those of competitors who don't use visuals.

Sometimes it is not advisable to use sophisticated visuals. For example, if your company is downsizing or cutting costs, it would not be advisable to spend (or even appear to have spent) thousands of dollars on a professionally created presentation about ways to save money and decrease costs. Similarly, an audience without much experience listening to presentations might be distracted by elaborate visuals and slick transitions. They might spend more time looking at the visuals than really listening to your message. These decisions are often part of your audience analysis during your preparation.

TYPES OF VISUAL AIDS

There are many types of visual aids, and your selection will depend on your purpose, your audience, your own skills, and your budget.

As is shown in Table 15.1, different types of visuals have varying advantages and disadvantages. Generally, visual aids that take more time to design and create are the easiest to use during a presentation, but they can often be the most expensive. Some visual aids, like flipcharts and actual objects, work best with small groups, while others, such as slides, work well with groups of any size. With very small groups, users often display visuals right on the screen of a notebook computer.

Again, your selection of the type of visual to use will be made during your presentation preparation process. You need to decide which type of visual will:

- Best support your goals and the audience's requirements
- Work within your time, space, and budget limitations
- Be accepted by your audience
- Be the most comfortable for you to use

Your corporate culture will also frequently dictate the type of visuals that you can and should use. Some companies routinely expect PowerPoint presentations and have all conference rooms wired for easy use of the computer projection system. Others prefer lower-tech overheads or even handouts.

PRESENTATIONS MAGAZINE

Computers and audiovisual technology are changing quickly in the information age. Material written for this book may be outdated six months after it's published. For those interested in the latest in audiovisual technology, as well as helpful hints for business presentations in general, visit the web site of *Presentations* magazine at www.presentations.com. Here you will find articles and tools from recent publications, upcoming trade shows, and subscription information. It's the latest, up-to-date information on presentation technology tools.

CHARACTERISTICS OF GOOD VISUAL AIDS

We have found that good visual aids for presentations have five general characteristics (see Table 15.2):

- Visible (easy to see)
- Errorless
- Easy to use

TABLE 15.1 TYPES AND CHARACTERISTICS OF VISUAL AIDS

Visual Aid	Cost	Equipment Rental
Computer-created and projected slides	High initial investment in computer and software	Computer and projection system needed
Overheads or transparencies	Relatively low; prepare on computer or copy machine	Overhead projector, generally available
Photographic slides	Moderate cost for camera and processing film	Slide projector
Posters	Relatively low, cost of posterboard and markers	Easel to support poster
Handouts	Relatively low copy costs, unless using color	None
Objects	Low	None
Flipcharts (easels)	Low	Chart, easel, marking pens
Whiteboards	Low	Board and marking pens
Chalkboards	Low	Board and chalk

- Attractive
- Relevant

KEY CONCEPT A Good Visual Aid Is Visible

If your audience can't see your visual, it cannot be effective. Is this common sense? Yes. However, we still see visuals that are too small (overall) in size, have fonts that are too small, and incorporate poor color choices.

**TABLE 15.1
(CONTINUED)**

Technical Skill Needed	Advantages	Disadvantages
Competence in visual design and equipment use	Professional image, flexible design, special effects	Cost and equipment; may distract listeners
Competence in visual design; must learn to center and focus	Easy to use; can use and connect with audience	Needed equipment
Low; projectors work with remotes	Projects large and attractive images; works well with audio	Must darken room; lose contact with audience
Some artistic or computer design ability	Easy to use	Too small for large group
None	Helps listeners remember ideas	Can distract from message and speaker
None	Demonstration	May be too small to see
None	Good to record group ideas	Often messy and unprofessional
None	Flexibility to write spontaneously	Often messy and unprofessional
None	Flexibility to write spontaneously	Often messy and unprofessional; must turn back on listeners

Visuals That Are Too Small

You cannot create a good visual by simply typing up a list of ideas and using the list as a visual. Nor can you take a chart from a report, copy it onto a transparency or scan it into a software presentation package, and expect it to be visible to your audience. You have to anticipate the general size of the group you will be addressing and the general dimensions of the room you will be using in order to size your visuals appropriately. If the overall image is too small, it won't be effective.

TABLE 15.2 CHARACTERISTICS OF GOOD VISUAL AIDS

Visual Characteristic	Audience Concerns	Don't	Do
Is the visual aid visible?	Can they see it?	Use type smaller than 24-point, combine too many colors, use dark backgrounds with dark lettering	Check your visual aid in the room you will be using and with the equipment you will be using
Is the visual aid errorless?	Are they distracted by typos and inaccuracies?	Forget to proof, grammar and spell check	Proofread; get a colleague to proof; spell check; grammar check
Is the visual aid easy to use?	Are they distracted by the user's ineptitude?	Use a visual you aren't familiar with and technology you haven't practiced with thoroughly	Use the easiest and most convenient visual in keeping with your audience needs
Is the visual aid attractive?	Can they understand the point of the visual? Is it nice to look at?	Put too much on one slide, use complete sentences, use too many colors, use fluorescent colors	Use a simple design; use key-word bulleted text; use a few primary colors; use a consistent template or company logo
Is the visual aid relevant?	Does it tie directly to the topic and enhance their understanding of the message?	Use irrelevant pictures or clip art, use humorous images without careful consideration	Use only the best supporting materials to enhance your argument

Visuals with Small Fonts

Another common, avoidable problem is the use of fonts that are too small. For most rooms, a good rule of thumb is that the smallest font on your visual should be 24 points, with appropriately larger sizes to emphasize the differences among your heads and subheads (see Chapter 5 on Layout and Design). However, be aware that even some fonts that are recommended in some computer software templates may not be large enough or clear enough when used in a projector. (See Figure 15.1.)

Visuals with Poor Color Choices

Choosing the specific color(s) to use in your visuals is a complex task. You need to consider, among other factors, your company or corporate image. Are there spe-

The presenter used the High Voltage design from PowerPoint, which was an appropriate template for the presentation. The font, Impact, looked good on the computer screen. However, when it was projected on the big screen and video-taped for the local cable station, the letters ran together.

The presenter easily corrected the problem by changing the font from Impact to Arial, thereby creating a much more readable visual that was more clear on the videotape of the presentation.

FIGURE 15.1 *Problems with font.*

cific color combinations that are identified with your company (e.g., red for the Xerox logo; yellow for Eastman Kodak's film boxes; green for Fuji film)?

You also need to consider your audience's cultural background. In some cultures, white is a sign of happiness and celebration; in others, it is a sign of mourning.

We know of one major multinational company that had to repackage a product line because it used the wrong colors; the same thing can happen to your presentation. It can fail simply because you didn't choose the right colors or because you chose colors that didn't work well together.

For example, red letters on a blue background might look cool on your computer screen, but the combination is hard to read on a projection screen. Be sure to test your materials *before* your presentation.

A Good Visual Aid Is Errorless

KEY CONCEPT You need to do more than just run your slides' text through the spell checker. A spell checker typically doesn't highlight misused words. You must proofread carefully, more than once, and ask a colleague to proofread for you, too. It is very hard to pick up your own errors, and these become magnified when shown to a group on the big screen. Any numbers or charts should be double-checked for accuracy, and confirm that your percentages add up to 100 percent. We guarantee that someone in every group will notice and point out such errors, casting doubt on your credibility (even if the information came from someone else).

A Good Visual Aid Is Easy to Use

KEY CONCEPT Choose a medium with which you are comfortable and that is readily available in your business settings. Using readily available overhead projectors might make more sense than renting and setting up a computer projection system.

A Good Visual Aid Is Attractive

KEY CONCEPT We have found that some visuals are easier to look at than others. An attractive visual that combines a few primary colors in an appropriate way is preferable to using all 16 million colors on your palette. Stay away from florescent shades that scream "Look at me!" and distract from the message. Beyond color, the design should be clear, uncluttered, and consistent (for example, your company logo might appear in the same location on each slide). What you are trying to show on the visual should be immediately apparent to your audience. The diagrams and figures should not be so complex and convoluted that your audience is confused or has trouble following the idea.

Additionally, you should not try to get too much on one visual. Rather than four pie charts on a single visual, show them separately to focus the audience's attention. If you want to show a comparison of the four, introduce them individually and build a slide to bring them together later.

Figure 15.2 provides an example of how to design more attractive visuals. For guidelines on using color, see Chapter 5 on layout and design. Also check out our web site at ron-hein.com for more examples.

Good Visual Aids Are Directly Relevant

Your visuals should be directly relevant to your topic, and they should not distract from your purpose and focus. Even if you spent hours collecting data, you don't have to show every statistic if it doesn't directly support your point or if your audience doesn't need to know about it.

Getting Cute

There are several things your visuals should generally avoid, including cartoons, humor, and irrelevant photos or clip art. Cartoons and other humorous materials can be effective under some circumstances, but they can also be offensive. Use them judiciously. Resist the urge to scan irrelevant photos and clip art into your presentation just to jazz up a text slide. If a piece of art or a photo doesn't have a direct link to your topic, it will distract the audience from your presentation. Although you may have the world's cutest kitten, Muffin's picture doesn't belong in your presentation—unless, perhaps, you work for Purina.

GUIDELINES FOR USING VISUAL AIDS

There are three basic guidelines for using visuals effectively: Practice with your visual aids, show your visual at the right time, and maintain maximum eye and voice contact with the audience.

Practice with Your Visual Aids

Before you stand up to deliver your presentation:

- Know how to use the audiovisual equipment.
- Know what to do if the equipment isn't working.
- Have a backup plan if you can't run the the audiovisual technology or it cannot be repaired.

Also, keep in mind:

- When you will put up each visual

Manufacturing Costs, 1998

In 1998, 15% of our costs went for labor, materials were 35%, overhead was 45%, and depreciation was 5%.

Poor. Too wordy, data embedded in text, not set up for easy comparison.

Manufacturing Costs: 1998

- Labor: 15%
- Materials: 35%
- Overhead: 45%
- Depreciation: 5%

Improved. But numbers are not best represented by bulleted text.

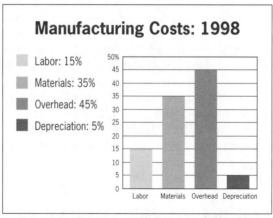

Good. Bar chart clearly shows how the figures compare.

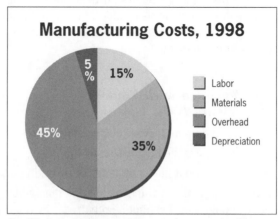

Good. A pie chart is another good way to show proportional figures.

FIGURE 15.2 *Development of a visual aid.*

- When you will take it down
- How to do so without blocking the projection of the visual or your audience's view of it

 Show Your Visual Aids Only at the Right Time

Audiences are easily distracted, and because they tend to look at visual aids, you need to be sure your audience's attention is on an appropriate, relevant visual.

When you (and your audience) are done with a visual, take it down, and don't put up the next visual until you are ready. Correct timing of your visuals is essential if you are going to retain control of your presentation and keep your audience focused on your purpose and message. When using overheads, it is acceptable to leave the screen blank in between transparencies; on a computer system, insert a blank slide or a title slide into the presentation.

 Don't use the automatic timer on your computer projected visuals. It may be tempting to use this technology tool to have your visuals advance automatically. However, in an extemporaneous presentation, you may change your phrasing, add new examples, or change the pace of your talk. It's always better for you to control the timing of the slides.

 Maintain Maximum Eye and Voice Contact with the Audience

A competent speaker has control over his or her audience. In order to maintain this control, you should keep your eyes and voice focused on the audience as much as possible. This is why the chalkboard is a poor visual aid: It requires the speaker to turn away from the audience to write, and thus contact with the audience is lost. Even if you stand sideways, you are still seeing and connecting directly with only half your audience. Many people make this same mistake with overheads and slides. They turn their backs to the audience and point and talk to the screen. Use a pointer and touch the transparency/overhead in order to identify key areas. With a projection system, learn to use the cursor or program's pointer. You might also use a laser pointer, but don't try these without sufficient practice, as they are tricky to control properly.

 Avoid the "slow reveal" with overheads. You've no doubt seen people try to do a "slow reveal." When displaying a list of points on an overhead, they cover up the list with a piece of paper and reveal key points one line at a time.

Not only is this process awkward and distracting, it also is extremely patronizing to your audience. If you truly think your complete message will distract your listeners, try one of the following:

- Build the final visual by adding overlays.
- Use separate visuals.
- Use a computer program (for example, PowerPoint) to display slides in a sequential and timely fashion.

END POINT

Visual aids can greatly enhance your message and help your audience comprehend and retain that message. Before you get up in front of your audience, remember to check your visuals by putting them up and testing them. Make certain you can see them from the back of the room, or a similar room, with the lights set at the appropriate level.

You, the speaker, need to consider your visuals throughout the phases of the prepresentation process. Use audience analysis, supporting materials, and your own experience and corporate culture as guidelines for choosing the most effective visual. Be sure to practice your presentation with your visuals, so you can be certain they support and advance the points you are trying to make. As you practice, you can also double-check your visuals for visibility, accuracy, attractiveness, and ease of use. Finally, have a backup plan in the event you experience an audiovisual breakdown.

These guidelines for the design and use of visual aids will help to improve your presentation and add impact to your message.

Fast **F**orward to the Real World

Using Audiovisual Technology in Presentations

The following interview was conducted with Nicholas Marinaccio, Media Presentation Specialist at St. John Fisher College on October 19, 1998.

Microphones and Sound Systems

Let's start at a very basic level, with a piece of audio equipment not many people think about, the microphone. If I am addressing a large group and need to use a microphone, what kinds of things do I need to know?

If it's a large room that needs a sound system, you first want to know if there is a sound system there and, if not, what it will take to get one there. After all, if the audience can't hear you, you won't have a chance to make a good presentation.

Once you have a sound system, it's just a matter of your presentation style. Your options are a wireless lavaliere mic or body mic, or a portable handheld, which can either be used away from the podium or kept at the podium on a mic stand. If you're a wanderer, and don't stay behind a podium, you want a wireless mic that allows your hands to be free.

What kinds of mistakes do people make with a podium mic?

People don't come to the room and practice beforehand. When one of our professors had to read the names for commencement last year, he came the day before to rehearse, so he could get a feel for the environment and see if there was a monitor where he could hear himself. That's a treat for both the sound engineer, who can iron out any problems, and also for the speaker, who is able to get a feel for the room and the environment.

Beyond practicing, a general rule of thumb is to point the mic at your chin. I've seen people reading from a paper with the microphone pointed to their forehead, and they read to the podium; and no one can hear them.

You mentioned remote or wireless microphones. If I am given a remote mic, where is the best place to put it?

It sometimes depends on the microphone, but generally right on the chest cavity. If it is not over the chest cavity it won't pick up as well, because the chest cavity is a resonator. You can feel the spot vibrating when you speak if you put your hand there.

(Continued)

(Continued)

Where do I put the battery pack?

The wire is fished up through the shirt or jacket and the mic comes out where a tie clip would go. The battery pack comes out at your hip or waist and can be clipped at your side or back.

Anything else speakers should know about sound systems?

Feedback is something to be aware of, especially if you're free and able to roam. You should take note of where the speakers are placed, because if you walk in front of them with the microphone on, you will cause feedback. If you do hear feedback, just move away.

Computer Projection Systems

Most PCs today come with Microsoft Office, which includes PowerPoint for designing visual aids. What do people need to know about using PowerPoint or other presentation software for their presentations in terms of needed equipment?

First, they need to know how to use the software and how to design the visuals so they will help the presentation. People make mistakes like putting their entire text on PowerPoint or designing slides that people can't see because of color or font or size. Actually, all the equipment you need is a computer and a compatible projector.

What kind of an investment would it take to purchase or rent a computer projection system?

Almost any computer can be used for projection as long as it is compatible with the projector. To rent a projector for a day is about $250, but to buy them would cost anywhere from $3,000 to $60,000 (and beyond). If you had to start from scratch, with a small projector and a laptop for mobility, you could probably get away with a $5,000 investment.

How hard is it to hook up my computer to the projection system?

A lot of the projectors coming out today are very user-friendly. The presenter doesn't have time to learn the hardware inside and out. So what they've done is try to simplify the projectors to the point where you just plug them in and they work. Some have a preconfigured cable, called a *smart cable,* which has a foolproof dial. When turned to PC, it gives you the PC ports; turn the dial to MAC, and it has the MAC ports you need.

Once you've designed your slides and you're set up with your equipment, what is the most important thing to know?

The cardinal rule for presentations: Always have a backup! Keep a spare set of transparencies or other visual images on hand in case of a computer failure or power failure. People are so dead set on using the com-

(Continued)

(Continued)

puter-generated presentation for dramatic effect, but they must realize that it's not worth wasting time waiting for someone to either fix the problem or restore power.

Actually, for one of my workshops, I had a PowerPoint disk with backup overheads, and we had a power failure. Luckily, I had printed out the slides in PowerPoint's Handout mode, so I had something to give out. It didn't have the same impact, but at least we didn't have to cancel the entire session.

It's just not worth worrying about it and becoming flustered. That can really affect your whole presentation.

Other than power failures, is there ever a time when you'd advise a speaker not to use a computer projection system and just use overheads or transparencies?

A professor was making a presentation at a local bookstore and wanted to use a computer-based presentation. In the end, it was quicker just to use a flipchart and a marker, because the presentation was one in which she would be adding diagrams to depict different situations, depending on what questions were asked. If she had used PowerPoint, she would have had to spend massive amounts of time making up slides showing every possible situation. Sorting through all those possibilities would have hindered the presentation. With experience using computer visuals, she may have been able to pull it off. But this was not the time to rewrite her presentation.

For a smaller audience a flipchart can work well too, because people can see it . . .

There's the ability to answer a question on the spot and demonstrate it by drawing the diagram. She could adapt her answer more easily and demonstrate it using a visual.

Are there any other situations where the computer might not be the best choice?

Small groups where you have everyone's attention. If you have an intimate presentation where there are only three or four people, a handout they can take with them in full color can work just as nicely as a Power-Point presentation. It might even be better, because they all have the same notes in front of them; they look through it with you; and they can keep it for future reference.

Could some parts of PowerPoint actually be distracting to the audience?

Too many different transitions are a presentation no-no; they are too distracting. The same rule applies in video—too many special effects distract your audience. Transitions should feel natural. Adding special effects because they are available looks amateurish.

(Continued)

(Continued)

Videotaped Presentation and Visual Aids

Since you've mentioned video, another area of concern is the situation in which the computer presentation is being videotaped, or the presentation is a part of a videoconference or even a live feed. We've seen some bad situations in which community meetings are being taped to show on the local cable TV station. What happens to the image as the computer projection is being videotaped? Is there anything you can do to enable the viewer to see the presentation clearly?

This is tricky, because you would think if you have a program you're going to deliver for television, you would set it up in a television atmosphere. In a television studio they could use a switcher to switch from the presenter to the actual presentation (slides directly from the computer). If there's something being made specifically for television, it's made in a studio, but that's not possible for a live presentation. If a studio-type recording isn't possible, the camera operator needs to position the camera so that the presenter and the presentation are shown. Unfortunately, you may get scan lines from the presentation, which can be distracting. Also, be aware of lighting. If it's light enough to see the speaker, it often isn't dark enough to see the slides.

Can the presenter do anything in designing slides to make more them more visible on videotape?

Background colors are important—white and black are good background colors. If the presentation gets busy, it becomes distracting. Contrast background color with foreground text and pictures.

Can you still get a good image?

When you videotape any computer screen you will get scan lines. There are ways around that, but it's not going to go away. I like to train the camera on the slide and leave the speaker's voice in the background.

The Internet and Presentations

How has the Internet changed the nature of the way presentations are given?

With the Internet, you can share information much more easily, often avoiding a physical meeting altogether. A presenter could actually convert a PowerPoint presentation to HTML-based format for the web.

Would this be just our slides, or are you saying you would actually be speaking?

Using the Internet, you could put up just your slide show for people to view. Some of the newer programs also allow you to add narration to your slides. It doesn't give the same impact as you giving your presentation, because your slide show shouldn't be your whole presentation.

(Continued)

(Continued)

But the Internet has given people the ability to share information more easily.

Other New Technologies

What other new technologies will impact how we make presentations?
Better and brighter-resolution projectors are coming out all the time, so the quality of the images will continue to improve.

With computers, everything is getting faster, while software is getting easier to use. There are more design options. In some cases, you can even get writing assistants that help you draft your presentation and documents. Software is getting "smarter."

Digital cameras are coming down in price and are being designed to be more versatile, so it will be easier to include images in your presentation slides.

Also, video editing equipment is becoming more affordable. It can be used in cross-computer platforms—with either a PC or a Mac. People used to lean toward one computer platform or another depending on what they needed to do. Generally, word processing was done on a PC, and graphics were done on a Mac, but now, software programs are being written for both platforms.

All of these developments have made life for the presenter a lot easier and, potentially, a lot more creative.

16

Practicing Your Delivery

When many people think about public speaking and business presentations, they think primarily of delivery skills. Indeed, many speakers initially think their biggest concern is how they look, sound, and act in front of a group of people. In truth, while delivery skills are important, they're secondary to defining your purpose, analyzing your audience, and organizing your ideas. At the same time, we recognize that competent delivery skills are essential to getting your message across to your audience. In this chapter, we discuss some of the more common concerns about delivery:

- Types of delivery
- Avoiding distractions
- Using your voice effectively
- Using posture and gestures to enhance your message
- Practicing your presentation

KEY CONCEPT — TYPES OF DELIVERY

There are four basic styles that you may use to deliver your presentation. We'll discuss each, and you'll find a brief summary of them in Table 16.1.

Reading from a Manuscript

While manuscripts for speeches may be acceptable for heads of state and Supreme Court justices, who must be precise in their content and wording, they are taboo in your everyday business presentations. Reading the text of a speech sets up a barrier between you and the

TABLE 16.1 TYPES OF DELIVERY

Style of Delivery	Advantages	Disadvantages
Manuscript	Precise wording, phrasing	Creates barrier with audience; limits eye contact/connection
Memorization	Precise wording, phrasing	Sounds recited; a disaster if you lose your train of thought
Impromptu	Helps you think on your feet	Not enough preparation for major presentation
Extemporaneous	Sounds conversational; allows adaptation to time/situation	Requires planning and rehearsal

audience; it limits the connection you can make personally with the audience; and it is generally frustrating to listeners, who would rather read the report themselves than hear you read it.

Having said that, we also recognize that high-profile speakers (heads of state, national newscasters, and corporate CEOs) can be effective when they read prepared scripts because of their control over the presentation context. They can position their audience and the TV cameras. They also use sophisticated TelePrompTers that project the text onto transparent viewing screens. The audience doesn't see these screens, so the speakers seem to make continuous eye contact. For the business presenter with a face-to-face live audience, however, we find that reading usually appears unprofessional and can damage the speaker's credibility. (See Table 16.2).

Speaking from Memory

You might choose to memorize your presentation, but we don't recommend it. There are two pitfalls: First, your presentation can sound stilted, as if you were reciting to the audience; and second, if you forget even one word or phrase, your mind can go blank and you will be lost (and, unlike your school play in second grade, there won't be a teacher in the wings to prompt you!). If you do choose to memorize, make sure that you work on the phrasing and intonation to avoid making your presentation sound like a recitation, and make sure you have a set of notes to back you up.

Impromptu Speaking

There are times when you will be called upon to speak off-the-cuff. You may be in a meeting and be asked to

TABLE 16.2 ABOUT WRITING SPEECHES

Many public speaking texts and instructional videos use the term "writing your speech" to describe the process of preparing and delivering a presentation. You won't find that term used here. We find that the most successful presenters do not write out a speech word for word and read it to the audience. Rather, the successful presenters research and organize their material, then speak extemporaneously, working from key-word notes and aiming for more conversational phrasing.

When are speeches written out and read?

Under some special circumstances, speeches are written out. For example, major policy and political addresses must be precisely worded and require a more formal delivery style. Similarly, keynote addresses at conferences may be successfully written out and read to a large audience. But most business presentations are delivered in the context of small meetings, often with fewer than 15 people present, and reading these presentations would be disastrous to your professional image because it would create a barrier between you and the audience.

Ghostwritten speeches

Sometimes, CEOs and high-level executives have someone else write their speeches so that they can allocate their time to more pressing business concerns. However, as a good speaker, you still need to guide the writer by clearly defining your key objectives and sharing your analysis of the audience. After receiving a draft of a ghostwritten speech, it is important to review, edit, and rehearse it, not only to be sure that the message accurately reflects your feelings and positions, but also to make certain that the words and phrasing match your personal style.

update the group on the status of your project, even though that wasn't on the agenda. Or you may feel compelled to speak up at a meeting when you have a strong opinion on a particular topic.
Keep the following tips in mind:

- Know your goal.
- Think quickly about the sequence of your points.
- Jot down one or two key words.
- Be concise.
- Make certain this specific setting is where you can most effectively make and sell your point.

Avoid an impromptu approach to major presentations. Your major presentations need to be planned, organized, and rehearsed before delivery. Even the best speakers need to plan ahead. (See Table 16.3 for an interesting exercise.)

TABLE 16.3 THE VALUE OF IMPROMPTU SPEAKING

Sometimes in public speaking classes, presentation skills workshops, and seminars, participants specifically practice impromptu speaking. Typically, speakers suggest topics and then draw them out of a hat or choose them on the spur of the moment. Each person stands up in front of the group and speaks for a minute or two on that topic. The results are often humorous and the content is rarely meaningful. One speaker might describe "my most embarrassing moment." Another might instruct the group on "how to brush and floss your teeth." Still another might offer thoughts on "who will win the Super Bowl this year." (This last one is particularly funny when the speaker knows nothing about the game of football.) But this exercise is not done just for laughs. The experience of speaking on an impromptu basis helps speakers learn to think on their feet and to practice speaking quickly and effectively.

Speaking Extemporaneously

When you speak extemporaneously, you're relying on a plan and key-word notes. This is the delivery style that we recommend. To do it successfully, you have to plan, determine your purpose, analyze your audience, and establish supporting materials. (See Table 16.4.) Rather than scripting your presentation, organize your ideas in a key-word outline, and then deliver your presentation from the outline or note cards. Aim for a conversational style, as if you were speaking to your audience in a one-on-one setting.

The unique feature of an extemporaneous presentation is that, if you were to deliver it several times, it wouldn't come out exactly the same way each time. With an extemporaneous delivery style, you can feel free to add thoughts and examples that occur to you during the presentation—or even eliminate some points if there's a time crunch. You have flexibility, and you can better involve and make connections with your audience. It's far more effective than reading, memorizing, or speaking in an impromptu manner, and your message will have maximum impact.

 AVOIDING DISTRACTIONS

In *Business and Professional Speaking,* published in 1983, and still very relevant today, Eric Skopec advocated a style of delivery that he called "mechanically adequate."[1] A mechanically adequate speaker does nothing to distract the audience from the message. So, rather than coming up with a long list of dos and don'ts for presentation delivery, each speaker can examine his or her own attributes and abilities in order to eliminate any distractions.

TABLE 16.4 EXTEMPORANEOUS SPEAKING

Extemporaneous speeches are:

- Prepared
- Outlined
- Researched
- Rehearsed
- Conversational
- Flexible

Advantages of extemporaneous speeches:

- Personal connection with audience
- Adapt to time limits
- Flexibility with audience feedback

Unique features of extemporaneous speeches:

- You can deliver it any number of times and it won't come out exactly the same way each time.
- You, the presenter, have control over the presentation situation.

For example, many people find they speak more quickly when they are nervous, as one might be in a public speaking situation. Speaking too quickly can distract from your message because your articulation can suffer and audience comprehension can be diminished if you don't allow time to let the ideas sink in. Eliminating such a distraction from your delivery allows the audience to focus on the message.

It is important to identify and eliminate common distractions, including those associated with your appearance, gestures or repetitive actions, and posture (videotaping and peer critiques work wonders!). A busy combination of colors, an open fly, too much makeup and jewelry, and an unkempt appearance can all distract the audience from your message. Playing with your pen and jingling the change in your pocket may not be noticeable to you, but they are to the audience. Even a stiff posture with no movement can call attention to itself.

It's helpful to think about network news broadcasters. While there may be a few exceptions, we generally don't know where they're from by their dialects; we don't recall specific outfits; and we don't remember if they used any special posture or gestures. Broadcasters avoid distractions so that you, the audience, can focus on the news story. And that is the goal in presentational speaking. You don't have to try to be John F. Kennedy,

Barbara Jordan, or James Earl Jones. Your job is to be yourself, to deliver your message, and to avoid distracting your audience from that message.

USING YOUR VOICE EFFECTIVELY

Most people are rather surprised when they first hear themselves on tape. "Do I really sound like that?" We don't have a good sense of how we sound to others because the structure of the ear and its vibrations interfere with how we perceive our own voices. If you don't like your voice, there isn't a whole lot you can do to change its quality. You can, however, make sure that your voice doesn't distract from the message.

Practice

Practice your presentation, or even read a passage from the newspaper, using a cassette recorder. (Don't use a video camera, because you might be distracted by your appearance and other aspects of nonverbal communication.) Listen to your tape for the following:

- Is your articulation crisp and sharp, or do you drop endings and run words together? The appropriate use of a simple *-ing* ending (for example, speakin' versus speaking) can make the difference between sounding competent or unprofessional.

- Is your tempo appropriate for easy listening, or do you speak too quickly or too slowly? Is your voice too loud or soft for the size of the room and the audience?

- Does your voice sound expressive? Are you demonstrating that you understand the meaning of the message, or are you speaking in a monotone, as if you're just reading or reciting something of no interest?

- Do you use vocal "fillers" that might distract from the message? Once the audience starts counting your "ums," you're in trouble and probably don't even realize it.

Your own self-analysis, or that of a close friend or coworker, can help you identify one or two areas to improve before your next presentation.

One way to solve a pesky delivery problem is to exaggerate the solution when you practice. Let's look at two examples:

- *Speaking too quickly.* If you speak too quickly and run your words together, a potential solution is to practice speaking very slowly and distinctly. At first, make your speech agonizingly slow. Force yourself to slow down and articulate each word. As you start to speak more distinctly, gradually speed up to a more normal pace.

- *Speaking in a monotone.* If you sense that your voice is too monotone and expressionless, try emulating a dramatic actor. For a few minutes, get crazy with your message. Have some fun. Exaggerate the changes in your pitch and intonation. Then gradually calm it down and use your audience analysis information to determine what changes will improve your presentation style.

Make certain, however, that you eliminate these extreme "practice exaggerations" from your actual presentation style. We have encountered one exasperating and pretentious presentations instructor who gains attention in groups, meetings, and presentations by using overly dramatic intonations. Not only are such exaggerations aggravating, they are also distracting and counterproductive. When you are delivering your presentation, avoid being egocentric, and pay attention to feedback from your audience. They'll know the difference between your acting a dramatic role and just being yourself.

Getting Rid of Those Vocal Fillers

Eliminating vocal fillers (for example, *um, uh, well, like,* and *ya know*) can be the toughest challenge facing some speakers. Typically, the best technique is to spend time consciously trying to get rid of them. You should not wait until the day of the presentation and write yourself a note: "Don't say *um!*" It won't work.

Get rid of the *ums* by consciously eliminating them during casual conversations at the dinner table or with friends. By eliminating these fillers from your casual conversation you will be able to get rid of them in your business presentations.

 ## USING POSTURE AND GESTURES TO ENHANCE YOUR MESSAGE

Now it's time for you to get out that video camera or stand in front of a mirror. Deliver your presentation or do an impromptu self-introduction while watching your behaviors. A good presenter maintains eye contact with the audience, presents pleasant facial expressions, has an upright but not stiff posture, and uses gestures to emphasize points. For most business presentations, your audience is relatively small, and you don't need the dramatic gestures and movement that would be appropriate on a stage in front of thousands. To enhance your message, use these two guides:

- Appear natural and relaxed, as you would in most business discussions. Remember, it's okay to smile.
- Use nonverbal communication cues to add emphasis to your message.

Because your gestures, posture, and even voice intonations can affect the quality of your presentation, it's important to be aware of how you're projecting to your audience. The following suggestions can help you do this.

Make Eye Contact

You want to maintain eye contact with the audience by looking at one person for several seconds, then moving on to another person. Don't read from your notes, although it's okay to glance down at them occasionally.

If you try to avoid looking at your audience by looking beyond them (to the clock on the back wall, for example), people will notice and become distracted—and to you the audience will seem like an intimidating mob.

If you quickly glance around the room and do not maintain eye contact while you make your point, you're using the "scared rabbit" approach. Darting eyes make you appear to be extremely nervous.

Remember, you are under no obligation to look at everyone in the audience. If it works better for you, choose to focus on the friendliest faces, such as people who are nodding in agreement with your message.

However, don't ignore people who are starting to frown or look bored. They are giving you extremely important feedback, and you need to be aware of them before you get into questions and answers.

Use Appropriate Posture

Your posture should be professional and confident. In most situations, this means that you should stand firmly on two feet and not shift your weight from side to side or lean on a table or podium. Don't appear stiff and unnatural. Incorporate some movement into your delivery style, but don't pace or wander. You might move toward the overhead or computer in order to display visuals, or you might take a step toward your audience to emphasize a point. Use natural movements as you would when you are engaged in animated conversations.

Taking a step toward a listener who is starting to look bored (or worse, nodding off) can help that person become more attentive, and it can eliminate a major distraction to others who are trying to listen.

Make Your Gestures Work

Like your posture, your gestures should be natural and seem like a normal extension of your body language. One effective technique is to use your hands for emphasis, to punctuate your discussion, and to refer to your visual aids. For example, to help structure three points in your presentation, hold up one, then two, then three fingers to emphasize the sequence. If the gesture feels like a natural part of your presentation, it is probably appropriate.

DANGER! Avoid distracting, nervous, repetitive, and meaningless movements—for example, tapping on the podium, playing with your ring or watch or pen, jingling the keys or coins in your pocket, or stroking your beard. Speakers can generally identify their own distracting gestures after a brief encounter with a mirror or a few minutes of videotape. Again, you need to practice in order to get rid of those distractions.

KEY CONCEPT **PRACTICING YOUR PRESENTATION**

"Practice? Who has time to practice?" We hear that comment too often from managers, executives, and students when it comes to preparing for a presentation. Many executives feel such time pressure that they barely have time to gather their data and make a few slides before speaking. However, if you ignore this crucial step in the preparation of your presentations, you will surely find some surprises—and may even experience some of our "presentation disasters" (see Table 16.5). Practice alleviates speech anxiety, and being prepared is a courtesy to your audience members. The people listening to you are spending their valuable time, and you need to help them use it effectively.

Often, presenters don't know how to use successful techniques for practicing their speeches. Instead, they frequently take their note cards into a conference room and review them, sometimes quietly muttering the phrases they intend to use. This is rarely helpful because it is a setting and rehearsal very far removed from the actual presentation situation.

The following guidelines can help you more effectively practice your presentation:

- *Duplicate, as closely as possible, the conditions under which you will presenting.* Try to practice your presentation in the room where you'll be delivering the speech. If that's not possible, be sure to stand (unless your presentation calls for you to sit) and project your voice as if you were speaking to the number of people you expect.

TABLE 16.5 PRESENTATION DISASTERS

We've seen enough presentations in our years of teaching and consulting to get a good sense of what does and doesn't work with an audience. Here are some of our more memorable "presentation disasters."

- *Factual errors.* One group of MBA students who served as consultants to a local business not only got the name of the company wrong, they misspelled it on every slide. It should go without saying: Proof once, proof again, then get someone else to proof visuals for you. If you miss something as basic as the company name, your audience will start to wonder what else you might have missed.

- *Inappropriate attire.* We've seen everything from project engineers in scruffy jeans to executives in too-trendy clothing that included loud colors and short skirts. There is no single correct way to dress, but you should always appear professional and in sync with the rest of your team and with the audience. (If you mowed the lawn in those pants, they probably aren't right for a presentation.)

- *Really, really bad slides.* We thought we'd made the point about good visual aid content and design, but some people still insist on typing things up on a word processor, putting them on an overhead, and covering, then revealing, one line at a time to the audience. This drives us— and others—crazy! We were totally distracted from the content presented by a physician whose overheads were out of focus and caused eyestrain. If you want to use visual aids, be prepared to do it right. Make sure they are visible and that they enhance your presentation.

- *Condescending attitude.* Sometimes this happens because people really *are* smarter than the rest of us, and their impatience shows; more often, it's to make up for feelings of inadequacy or lack of confidence in the content. Either way, it puts off the audience and lessens a speaker's credibility and impact. If you're not sincerely interested in getting your message across, you are doomed to fail. Every single audience deserves respect.

- *Lack of preparation.* This is one disaster we've seen all too often. The audience resents lack of preparedness as an intrusion into their busy time. As a consequence, your image suffers. Even if you have great charisma, you can't charm your way out of a poorly prepared presentation. Block out the time you need to prepare and practice so you do your professional best.

- *Practice with your visual aids.* Nothing tries the patience of an audience as much as technical problems with visuals, and there is nothing more certain to heighten a speaker's level of anxiety. Use your visuals when you practice to make sure they work properly. Confirm that you have matched the timing and placement of visuals to the talking points of your presentation.

- *Practice with a tape recorder or a video camera.* Using a tape recorder or a video camera will give you an opportunity to hear how you sound and to critique your content and phrasing so that you can make any necessary adjustments ahead of time.

● *Practice in front of an audience, if possible.* It can be extremely helpful to have a coworker, colleague, friend, or spouse listen to you and comment on your presentation. People close to you want you to succeed and will be brutally honest in their evaluations if you ask them. Furthermore, if you can give your presentation to a family member with all the distractions of home about you, you should have no problem when it comes to the real thing.

END POINT

Delivering a presentation well is a matter of planning and practice. If you understand the types of delivery available and aim for an extemporaneous style, you will establish rapport with the audience and improve the likelihood of accomplishing your goal. Concentrate on avoiding any behaviors or mannerisms that would be distracting to your audience. Use your voice and gestures to enhance your message. Finally, *practice.* It is the key to improving your delivery style, enhancing your confidence, and increasing your chances of success.

Even if you need to improve in a few areas, don't panic. Work on one or two areas at a time. Major improvements seldom come overnight. Remember, your initial goal is be mechanically adequate, to do nothing that distracts from your message.

Your goal is not to have people leave saying, "What a great speech!" Your goal is to have them saying, "What great ideas!"

Stellar Performer:
Practicing Your Delivery
Dr. William Pickett

When Dr. William Pickett became President of St. John Fisher College in Rochester, New York, in 1986, he brought a number of firsts to the formerly Catholic college. He was the first lay president in the history of the college, the first president to be involved in significant outreach to the community, and the first president to use his presentation skills to open up the process of leadership to the entire campus community.

One of Dr. Pickett's early institutions was the Annual State of the College address. "The President of the United States has a State of the Union, and many governors deliver a State of the State address," says Pickett. "Even the mayor of Rochester gives an annual State of the City address. This seemed like a good way to inform the trustees, faculty, staff, and students about what was happening at the College and what our plans for the future were." The process that Dr. Pickett used in planning and preparing his speech serves as a model for how any professional should prepare for a major presentation.

During the summer months, when the office routine slowed somewhat, Dr. Pickett began planning his address to be given in late September. "I first outlined the main points I wished to cover, and jotted down a few ideas under each," reports Dr. Pickett. "Then I circulated that outline to my senior staff for comments. After receiving their feedback, I began to outline my remarks, using outlining software to keep the ideas organized." As he drafted each section, Dr. Pickett would take it to the individual with expertise in that subject area to check for accuracy and make additions and deletions. Finally, when the entire draft was completed, he again circulated the full manuscript to the entire staff for final comments.

Dr. Pickett also made rehearsal an important part of his preparation. In addition to practicing on his own in order to become familiar with the content and phrases, he also practiced in the auditorium where the presentation would be delivered. "It was important for me to practice with the microphone to make sure I was comfortable with the sound system," he says. "In later years, as I incorporated visuals into my talk, I would practice with the slides and overheads. This helped my confidence because I knew everything worked properly and the timing was accurate."

One of his biggest delivery challenges was that he had to give a speech he knew would be published as a report to various constituencies of the College. "I realized that reading the text was not a very interesting way of presenting," says Dr. Pickett. "The last two or three years, I actually talked from an outline and tried to cover the material that was in the text. I think that improved the quality and liveliness of the presentation and still produced a text for publication."

(Continued)

(Continued)

On the day of the presentation, Dr. Pickett would leave the office at noon, go home, have something to eat, relax, and review his notes one final time. He arrived at the presentation focused on his agenda and thoroughly prepared.

Note: Dr. William Pickett is now the Director of Pastoral Planning for the Roman Catholic Diocese of Rochester, New York.

17

Handling Questions and Answers

The presentation is over. You've delivered your sure-to-win-them-over conclusion, and you heave a big sigh of relief. Not so fast.

How you handle the question-and-answer (Q&A) session following a presentation can be as important as what you do during the presentation itself. By preparing for your listeners' questions and maintaining control of those questions, you can add impact to your presentation. Without adequate preparation, you can undo everything your speech accomplished.

Preparing for questions occurs at several points during your preparation process. Even during the preparation step, when you analyze the audience and set your goals, you should anticipate questions that might arise. For example, if you know that one of your colleagues always raises objections to proposals based on long-term implications, you can be sure to project your data to cover the future impact. If your presentation depends heavily on explaining quantitative figures to nonquantitative people, you can test your figures and charts on a colleague beforehand. Not only will this give you the opportunity to prepare answers, you also can test those answers when you rehearse.

This chapter describes common pitfalls associated with answering questions and provides suggestions for using Q&A sessions to add strength and credibility to your presentation. We'll address the following:

- Preparing for questions
- Taking questions in a business presentation
- Listening effectively to questions

- Responding when you don't know the answer
- Maintaining control of the Q&A session
- Planting questions: Is this a good strategy?

PREPARING FOR QUESTIONS

Competent speakers prepare for question-and-answer sessions by anticipating questions during their preparation process. Politicians sometimes prepare for debates and press conferences by having their aides ask them the toughest questions they might face. If you are having trouble anticipating questions, try running your presentation (or its major points) past a colleague, or check with someone who will be attending the presentation and ask about their major concerns. By anticipating questions, you can be prepared not only to reply but also to have any needed backup information or data.

Although anticipating questions can be helpful, there is no substitute for thoroughly preparing your content. Public speaking textbooks often recommend that you gather three times as much information as you need for a presentation. Some of that added preparation will give you more knowledge and a higher comfort level on your topic, and much of it can be useful support in your question-and-answer session. Even if your presentation does not specifically cover the topic of a question, you might be able to use a piece of background information to satisfy your listeners and to demonstrate your competence on the topic.

TAKING QUESTIONS IN A BUSINESS PRESENTATION

Should you have the audience hold questions until the end, or should you take them during the presentation? There are pros and cons to both approaches.

Obviously, if you are doing an instructional presentation and your audience's understanding of subsequent material will depend on their understanding of earlier material, then you need to answer questions as they come up—or at internal summary points during your presentation.

When you use this technique, you need to make certain your audience isn't diverted from your main purpose and doesn't lose the thread of your message. Additionally, if you have strict time constraints, answering questions during your presentation may prevent you from completing the presentation.

By holding questions to the end, you may run the risk of not being able to address major concerns during the presentation. However, it may be worth the trade-off for a smooth, flowing talk delivered within your time constraints.

Let your audience know at the outset if they should ask questions along the way or hold them to the end of the presentation. Only you can decide which strategy works best, depending on your topic, audience, purpose, and time limits.

LISTENING EFFECTIVELY TO QUESTIONS

Many times, a speaker's listening skills suffer because of anxiety about delivering a major presentation. It's important to listen to questions carefully and to be prepared to respond with a quick, accurate, and appropriate reply.

When you are asked a question, make direct eye contact with the questioner and focus on the key words in the question. If you don't understand the question, ask for clarification (for example, you might say, "If I understand you correctly, you're asking . . .").

Be certain that you stay tuned in to the nonverbal communication that is associated with the question. A questioner's gestures, facial expression, and tone of voice can help you interpret the substance and tone of the message.

Do not fall into the trap of using rehearsed party-line responses. Politicians who answer every question with a rehearsed answer sound shallow. Be respectful of all questioners, and offer them an intelligent response.

Be certain to monitor your own gestures, facial expressions, and other nonverbal cues when you are both listening to questions and answering them. If you are on a team or panel, be attentive when others are speaking. Your inattention, even if you are preparing your own points, might be seen as an unintended sign of disrespect.

RESPONDING WHEN YOU DON'T KNOW THE ANSWER

If you haven't anticipated a question or you don't have the information, don't fake it! It is not worth the risk to your credibility as a speaker or as a manager to take a chance on information that might be wrong. The best approach is to indicate that you don't know the answer, and if it is important, tell the questioner you will find the answer and share it. If you believe someone else in the group has the information, you may refer the question to that individual; however, we recommend that you do so with caution—it is extremely easy to lose control of your presentation.

Remember, it is appropriate to point out, politely, that a question is not relevant and that the group needs to focus on the issues at hand.

MAINTAINING CONTROL OF THE QUESTION-AND-ANSWER SESSION

When you're the presenter, you're in charge, during both the presentation and the Q&A session. Several techniques will help you maintain control:

- Answer questions succinctly and nondefensively.

- Be informative rather than persuasive.

- Stick to the facts.

- Do not allow yourself to be drawn into a debate with a member of the audience.

The trick is to remember that when a question is asked, focus on the questioner, and when you respond, speak to the entire group. By including everyone in the reply, you will discourage the disruptive sideline chats that can occur while you are engaging one member and inadvertently excluding the rest of your audience. This technique can also help diffuse tension in a hostile situation.

When the allotted time is ending, or after you have answered major concerns, signal the close of your presentation: "We have time for only one more question." "My time is just about up."

There are two common mistakes speakers make during Q&A sessions. The first is forgetting to monitor the amount of time left. The second is failing to leave time for a brief concluding statement that will wrap up the session.

Ending the Q&A

In closing, you should shift the question-and-answer session back to your presentation topic in order to refocus your audience. Here's an example:

> *Thank you for your attention. I appreciate your interest in the new laser printer we have been developing, and I trust you'll continue your enthusiastic support of this venture. Please feel free to contact me with any additional concerns or ideas for strengthening the project.*

PLANTING QUESTIONS: SHOULD YOU DO IT?

We were surprised to learn that the instructor of a course on public speaking offered by a well-known organization suggested "planting" questions in the audience. Here's how it would work: A friendly coworker (or classmate) would ask what seemed to be a tough question; the speaker would then impress the audience (or the instructor) with a thorough response, sometimes backed up by additional visual aids.

Although planted questions have been alleged to occur at White House press conferences, this technique is seldom appropriate for a business setting (or any situation, for that matter). In fact, we consider the practice to be unethical.

Questions from the audience should be spontaneous. We don't advocate engineering a Q&A session in order to improve your image. Moreover, when it is apparent that a question is a setup, the speaker's credibility can become suspect.

END POINT

To a novice speaker, a question-and-answer session may seem like an intimidating situation, akin to a firing squad or an inquisition by a grand jury. It shouldn't be. A question-and-answer session is a positive opportunity for a speaker to advance the points made in the presentation and to clarify any areas of confusion. With the proper preparation, most speakers learn to welcome the Q&A and even enjoy the challenge.

CHAPTER 18

Handling Speech Anxiety

It's not all in your head. Speech anxiety is real. Survey after survey has found that the fear of public speaking is the most common fear that people have. More people fear giving a speech than are afraid of flying, spiders, or even death! If you are one of those who would rather visit the dentist than give a speech, you are not alone.

A little anxiety before a big presentation is normal, especially for high achievers, executive personalities. You can use that adrenaline to add energy and excitement to your message.

Although too much anxiety can get in the way of your doing a great job, our goal in this chapter is to help you understand and control speech anxiety by addressing the following two themes:

- Why are we afraid of public speaking?
- What can we do to reduce or control our speech anxiety?

 ## WHY ARE WE AFRAID OF PUBLIC SPEAKING?

You may have your own individual reason for being afraid of public speaking, but we can generally group the source of speech anxiety into one of three areas: fear of the unknown, a bad experience, and a social norm.

Fear of the Unknown

Think of your first day on a new job. You don't know what the work environment is like, how you'll be treated, or the sorts of responsibilities that you'll have. Once you become familiar with your work situation, a lot of those first-day jitters usually disappear.

It's the same way when you are making a presentation or giving a speech. Many people simply haven't had the opportunity to prepare and present speeches during their education and work experiences, and they are unfamiliar with the process and the outcome. They have not learned the steps involved in preparing for a business presentation, and they are unsure of how they should proceed. Additionally, since they have never delivered an oral presentation to a large group of people, they don't know how they personally will react to the situation or how it feels to have all those eyes staring at you.

A Bad Past Experience

A top MBA graduate student at the Simon School once related a personal experience in her Presentation Skills class. This student remembered the exact circumstances and even the exact words her fifth-grade teacher used to tell her she would never be a competent public speaker after one disappointing performance. For over 15 years this student had carried the stigma that she was a failure as a public speaker. She went on to overcome those self-doubts and become one of our finest speakers and a student government leader, but the sad truth is that many are not so fortunate.

Managers and executives often report that they had a defining bad experience in high school, a time when self-images are fragile and the need for peer acceptance is high. A single bad past experience may keep people from choosing professions or seeking out jobs that require professional communication skills. Similarly, long-held fears may cause an individual to miss chances for promotion to more responsible jobs that require presentations.

A Social Norm

If you watch young children performing a musical or dance number, they seem completely uninhibited. Flower girls in weddings rarely appear nervous, and children seldom ask you to turn off your video camera. We do not appear to be born with a fear of performing in front of others; it appears to be something that we learn somewhere along the way.

Perhaps we learn it from a parent who is nervous about a presentation at work, or from a teacher who tells her class, "Don't be nervous" as they get ready to put on a play for the school. It gets passed along when our college students tell their friends they have to give a speech and are greeted with, "Aren't you *nervous?* I could *never* do that!" In many ways, our culture has taught us to fear this event we call public speaking.

IS SPEECH ANXIETY REALLY A BAD THING?

In most circumstances, a little speech anxiety is good for you. It means that you are concerned about doing a good job and that you are conscientious about the message you need to deliver. A little anxiety gives you some adrenaline, some energy to put into your performance. People who are completely relaxed about giving a presentation tend to do a ho-hum job with their delivery. We need a little nervous tension in order to connect effectively with our audiences.

Conversely, when you have too much nervous energy, your anxiety can interfere with your presentation delivery. We next discuss strategies for overcoming your speech anxiety.

HOW CAN YOU REDUCE OR CONTROL YOUR SPEECH ANXIETY?

We believe that speech anxiety is real and that there are five excellent techniques for controlling or reducing it: knowing your material; practicing, practicing, practicing; knowing how you react; using visual aids; and reconceptualizing the situation. (We will also mention one technique that we *don't* recommend.)

Know Your Material

You don't have to have a Ph.D. to understand that people feel more comfortable talking about a subject they know well. Ask students who come unprepared for class and pray their teachers won't call on them. Even college professors will tell you they feel more comfortable discussing the subjects they know best rather than those that are less familiar and less frequently covered.

The more you know about your topic, the more comfortable you will feel in your presentation. When you are preparing a presentation and have the opportunity to pick your own topic, pick something you know and feel confident about. Be certain that you also choose a topic that relates to your audience (see Chapter 12).

If you can't pick your own topic, make sure you learn as much about it as you can during your preparation and drafting steps. Experts recommend gathering three times as much information as you need for your presentation. This will enable you to (1) pick only the best supporting material, (2) have a supply of backup information for the question-and-answer session, and (3) lessen your anxiety.

Practice, Practice, Practice

This step, which is part of your prepresentation process, is probably the single most important factor for alleviating speech anxiety. The more you practice, the more you will become familiar with the material and the more you will relax. But it isn't enough to simply review your notes or go through your prepared slides.

A good practice session needs to duplicate as closely as possible the circumstances under which you will give the presentation. This means practicing in the same room, or a similar room, in which your speech will take place, standing (if you will be standing for this presentation), and using the appropriate visual aids. (Review Chapter 16, "Practicing Your Delivery.")

Know How You React

Everyone has a different response to the pressure of a presentation situation, and only experience will teach you how *you* react. For the novice speaker, it may be startling just to stand at a podium with all those eyes looking at you. Others may find they have sweaty palms, a dry mouth, or trembling hands.

Identifying your own reaction is half the battle. Next, you need to take clear, logical steps to manage it. For a dry mouth, keep a noncarbonated beverage handy, and perhaps some hard candy or cough drops to suck on before you begin your presentation. For those of you who suffer from quivering hands, no one will notice unless you use your hand to point to a visual on the overhead projector, in which case, the image on the screen will magnify the shaking! To circumvent this problem, use a pointer or pen and place it firmly on the visual. As for sweaty palms, well, they won't really matter unless you shake hands with someone in the audience.

After you have taken steps to deal with your personal reactions, put them aside. Remember, an audience will only rarely perceive your level of anxiety. They are there to hear your message.

Use a Visual Aid

Visual aids (used judiciously, of course, as we suggested earlier) can also help reduce anxiety. While your audience is looking at a visual aid, they are not looking at you. If you feel pressured when you are the center of attention and have all those eyes staring at you, use a visual to focus their attention elsewhere momentarily and appropriately.

Reconceptualize the Situation
Put the audience first.

Most speakers become very self-oriented when they prepare for a speech. They worry about how *they* will look, how *they* will sound, how *they* will appear before the audience. The average business audience is not there to critique your public speaking style; they are there to hear your message.

To be successful and to help you ignore your nervousness, remind yourself: "I have a message I want this group to hear." Do not focus on the idea that you have to "perform" for this group.

Your audience analysis and the other steps you used to prepare your presentation will help you concentrate on your audience and how your message relates to them. When you do so, you will stop worrying about yourself and stop being nervous.

Similarly, you can think of the situation as an extended one-on-one conversation. Picture yourself sharing information with two or three key people in a casual conversation or small group discussion.

DANGER! *Don't imagine the audience in their underwear.* One of the most common tips you'll find in other books on public speaking is to relieve speech anxiety by imagining the audience in their underwear. This is *not* one we recommend.

The theory behind it is that if you can imagine the people in your audience looking silly, you won't feel so intimidated by them. We can't recommend this line of thinking because we work from the premise that good speakers need to respect their audiences and put those audiences first when conveying a message.

END POINT

Most people with speech anxiety will respond well with practice and thorough preparation. If, however, you feel that your own speech anxiety is more severe and that you require help beyond the tips provided here, we urge you to seek out an anxiety-reduction program. The success rate of these programs is excellent. Many speech departments and counseling offices at larger universities provide programs that generally use relaxation techniques and visualization skills to

TABLE 18.1 RESOURCES FOR PEOPLE WITH SPEECH ANXIETY

- Courses offered through local community and high school continuing education
- Toastmaster's International—available in companies and communities (check the phone book)
- Dale Carnegie Effective Speaking Programs
- Courses offered through local colleges for credit or noncredit
- Anxiety-reduction programs offered through universities or hospitals
- Private therapist or counseling
- Support groups for all types of anxiety disorders

help you learn to relax before and during a presentation.

Try one of these programs (see Table 18.1). It might make a difference in more than just your ability to make presentations!

Evaluating Your Presentation

As you're packing up your notes and visuals following your presentation, you probably feel a great sense of relief—and hopefully, a sense of accomplishment for a job well done. However, you shouldn't let these fleeting emotions be your final contact with this presentation. The best presenters add a final step to the process: a postpresentation evaluation. In this step, you evaluate each aspect of the presentation process and plan for future improvement. You need to do this specifically in three key areas: purpose, audience analysis, and delivery.

DID YOU ACHIEVE YOUR PURPOSE?

Early in the presentation process, you specified your general purpose, your specific purpose, and what you would like to have happen as a result of this presentation. Now you need to examine the outcome of your presentation: Did you achieve your purpose? Did you accomplish your goals for the presentation? If you did, why were you successful? If not, why not? What factors contributed to the audience's acceptance or failure of your proposal?

AUDIENCE ANALYSIS

If you followed a systematic presentation process, you probably spent a good bit of time doing audience analysis. You looked at what your audience knew, what you wanted them to know, and what they needed to know. How successful were you in reaching this particular audience? If you didn't reach them, why not? Go through the questions we asked you to explore in Chapter 12 to identify the source of the communication breakdown. Did the audience know more than you realized they knew? Were they bored by your presentation? Did they know less than you realized? Were they lost during your presentation? What might you have done differently to better connect with this group of people?

DELIVERY

This is probably the area most frequently used for a postpresentation evaluation. In this step, you evaluate the verbal and nonverbal communication that contributed to the success or failure of your presentation. Did you use your voice, posture, gestures, and facial expressions to maximum effectiveness? Did your visual aids work smoothly and enhance your presentation? Did you control your anxiety? Did you seem knowledgeable and confident in the question-and-answer session?

You may not be able to complete the postpresentation evaluation totally on your own. If you have a videotape of the presentation, this may help in your self-assessment. However, you may need to enlist the help of close colleagues to give you guidance on how well you met your objectives in the presentation. Certainly, if you are involved in a team project, team members should be open to constructive comments for improvement from others on the team.

One of our most memorable examples of thorough self-evaluation comes from a former MBA student at St. John Fisher College. Alan was an excellent presenter with a high-visibility job in county government, and he was always looking for ways to improve his performance. During his final presentation, he used a large poster board on an easel as a visual aid. When he was through referencing the chart, he took it down, as is appropriate. However, he hadn't decided what he was going to do with the chart. He held it awkwardly for a few moments and then laid it down on the floor. For a few moments, the audience could hear Alan's voice, but we saw only his back as he leaned down to lay his visual on the floor. It wasn't a major issue in what was otherwise an excellent presentation. However, when Alan saw the videotape, he was appalled by what he had done. Not only had he not planned how to remove his visual, he kept speaking while he lost visual contact with the audience. His written self-evaluation included two pages on the correct use of visual aids.

We aren't recommending that you get overly scrupulous about every aspect of your presentation delivery. However, you can be sure that Alan will never make that same mistake again. He evaluated his performance, didn't like what he saw, and developed a strategy for dealing with it in the future.

END POINT

Unless you evaluate your preparation and performance after the presentation, you won't be able to adjust your strategy for the next presentation. You may be condemned to repeat fatal errors or annoying distractions that can test the patience of your audience. Even if your presentation was successful in achieving your purpose, it is good to know just what you did correctly so you can capitalize on those strengths next time. Doing a presentation without systematic evaluation afterward is like not calling the doctor to find out if your child's throat culture is positive for strep: It leaves too much to chance and allows mistakes to multiply. The evaluation doesn't take long, and the insights will be well worth the effort.

Writing and Presenting as a Team

Because of the growth of teamwork and cooperative cross-functional projects in most business settings, managers and executives frequently find themselves working on group rather than individual projects. In Part 4, we show you how to manage group writing projects and team presentations, and we offer ways to apply both the writing and editing process and the presentation process to successful teamwork.

The Total Quality Management (TQM) movement and other leadership initiatives demand efficient group and team efforts. Executives need to manage group writing and presentation processes so that these processes consume less time and fewer resources. Managers also need to make decisions on the adoption and support of computerized software packages and tools designed for use by groups. The proper software tools and the right conceptual tools provide a team with an excellent structure for accomplishing its task.

Part 4 offers ways to adapt the writing and editing and presentations processes to team projects. We'll examine writing as a team in Chapter 20 and presenting as a team in Chapter 21. The implication is that you should complete your team writing project before you begin the team presentation process.

Writing a document and organizing a presentation as a team can be a frustrating experience, especially for those who prefer to write and present on their own. At the same time, an effective team can exploit the resources of its members and produce documents and presentations that are stronger, more coherent, and more persuasive than any one individual might produce alone.

Writing as a Team

When you are initiating team or workgroup projects with written products (for example, reports and proposals), it is important to start by implementing a writing and editing process parallel to the process described in Chapter 3. You need to focus on establishing a team process, evaluating team members' skills, and evaluating your written product.

STEP 1:
EVALUATE THE TEAM PROCESS

Plan ahead. Planning ahead, anticipating barriers, and analyzing strengths will help teams avoid wasted, redundant effort, which is a major reason that team projects exceed timelines and budgets. Does planning ahead sound simple? It is not. In fact, one of the first barriers that a team faces is the need to rein in compulsive team members who are driven to get their "real" work started, *immediately!*

For various team members, that "real work" might be writing down basic goals, developing a budget, designing research, allocating space for designing a prototype, or some other individual hot button.

Our hot button is saving time and eliminating redundant efforts, especially those related to writing up materials and developing databases. The quickest way to create work that will need to be redone is by having to rewrite. For a team project, these tasks range from the simple (deciding which word processing software to use) to the complex (establishing responsibilities, processes, and procedures for the complete project).

For writing projects, use these steps to improve the success of your team:

- Clarify the following:
    What needs to be done
    Who is doing it
    When they are doing it
    How they are doing it
    How long it will take
    What it will cost

- Use computers and software tools, such as:
    Word processing software
    Grammar and spell checkers
    Project management software
    E-mail
    Presentation software

- Edit drafts sequentially (see Chapter 3).

- Create a final document.

- Proof that final.

- Obtain appropriate releases (from content experts and managers).

- Plan how to reproduce and distribute the material.

- Distribute and reproduce the material.

- Follow up.

Begin by selecting a word processing package and a document template. Why? The minute that two or more people start to independently write up ideas, establish independent guidelines for project management, or choose different ways to handle data, the team will develop inconsistent products that will require revision after revision. Believe us! We have been there many times, and it is a monstrous headache and one common reason that team members end up working nights and weekends, editing and reediting, trying to get projects completed.

Prewriting steps will help you determine what you need to accomplish. We developed information on prewriting steps in Chapter 3, and we shared related information on defining your purpose in Chapter 11 and analyzing your audience in Chapter 12. Audience analysis is one of several prewriting steps, which include identifying your:

- Objectives or goals

- Users or readers (audience analysis)

- Users' objectives or goals

- Users' existing knowledge

- Users' questions and needs

Prewriting steps help you determine if writing is the appropriate or best technique to use in your situation, as well as what to include or exclude. To the extent you know what to include, who your audience is, and your goals, you will be able to avoid common initial writing errors and writer's block.

STEP 2:
EVALUATE YOUR TEAM

Evaluate and use team members' skills. We are assuming that the composition of a team has been determined and that you know what needs to be done. The next major step is evaluating who does what. A common problem that teams face is that people try to do tasks they are afraid to admit they cannot do. Not only is time wasted, redundant effort is needed to fix new problems that arise. Part 2 of this book addressed writing problems, and elsewhere (see ron-hein.com Grammar Workshops) we have developed materials that help managers and executives quickly identify and eliminate key writing problems. Keep in mind that people are often embarrassed to admit that they have weak writing skills, and sometimes they aren't even aware that there may be room for improvement.

To expedite projects, have the skilled team writers "write" and the skilled team editors "edit." Have team members complete tasks that best utilize their skills.

For projects with a major writing (and/or related presentation) component, we recommend that you follow these guidelines:

- Use a project leader and/or a study group leader.
- Know and share your own individual strengths and weaknesses.
- Anticipate personal and work-related problems and commitments (family, sanity, etc.) that may interfere.
- Summarize actions to be taken; assign responsibilities.
- Arrange useful, focused working sessions and times.
- Come prepared for work sessions.
- Follow through on assignments.
- Monitor and facilitate individual participation.
- Establish specific goals and timelines.
- Determine the format, layout, and templates for your written products first!

These simple yet often overlooked steps will greatly enhance your team productivity.

Use project managers. It is important to use project (or group) leaders to do the following tasks:

- Identify goals, products, and outcomes.
- Establish and coordinate timelines.
- Identify skill sets and other resources needed, such as content experts.
- Identify strengths and weakness of participants.
- Schedule and track the components of a project.
- Monitor progress and process concerns.
- Negotiate changes.
- Facilitate delivery of the project requirements and products.

Gantt and PERT charts are excellent tools for project management. We strongly urge you to use Gantt and PERT charts (even fairly simple ones) to identify and avoid conflicts related to allocation of resources (people, money, facilities, etc.) for specific projects and among multiple projects. Resolving conflicts among projects (and deciding which manager or senior vice president to please or put off) is a major headache.

Gantt and PERT charts are extremely useful for tracking related costs and testing what-if scenarios related to resource allocation. Problems often result from inadequate allocation of time and resources for completing research; writing and editing; printing and distributing materials; and preparing and practicing presentations.

In addition to Gantt or PERT charts, you may choose from a number of computerized project management software products (e.g., Microsoft Project). One problem, however, with project management software is that learning to use it is often a time-consuming task, and when a team is trying to ramp up a new project, that time is often not available.

Managing team projects is becoming more sophisticated due to the number of new options in word processing and project management software packages. It's useful for all managers to look at groupware packages (for example, Lotus Notes, Microsoft Project, Timeline) to determine how to share schedules and documents. It is seldom cost-effective to have your technical staff format documents and presentations. Avoid having highly paid executives or managers doing these tasks. In fact, after your content experts complete their initial drafts, hire a consultant or assign a highly skilled staff member to edit and format the materials.

 **STEP 3:**
EVALUATE WRITTEN MATERIALS

In addition to evaluating your process and team members' skills, you will be more successful in developing useful written materials if you have the following:

- An executive summary that can be used to make a decision
- A clear, logical organizational structure
- Visually emphasized key points
- Graphics, tables, and figures that advance your arguments and decrease text
- The substance of your report in body of the report, not in the appendixes
- A good conclusion
- Report(s), handouts, and visuals that are coordinated for your presentation

END POINT

If you follow the straightforward steps in this chapter, your written materials will be improved. To save time, develop any presentations based on your materials *after* you finish your written project. Having a finished document before you start to develop a presentation will lead to coordinated materials and fewer revisions of your presentation.

Presenting as a Team

Team presentations may derive from written documents or they may be initiated solely as stand-alone projects, without previously written documents as guidelines. Obviously, preparing a presentation from an existing document will give you a head start.

A TEAM PRESENTATION FROM A TEAM-WRITTEN DOCUMENT

If your assignment is to present a written document as a team, you've already tackled the biggest part of the job: defining your purpose, analyzing your audience, organizing your ideas, and gathering supporting materials. And you have probably worked on the layout and design of visuals where appropriate. So the first four steps of the presentation have already been completed. However, as a team, you need to review these steps to make sure everyone is working from the same game plan. Once you have done this, you need to do some very specific work to transform that document into an oral presentation. Some of the issues you need to work through with your team are as follows:

- *What material will we select for presentation?* A team presenting a report or proposal can rarely cover the entire document in an oral presentation. If you were to assume the audience members would also be reading the document, what are the most significant things that you would select to highlight for the presentation?

- *What format will we use to present the material?* Sometimes, past experience and/or corporate culture will tell you how to present the material. At some companies, presenters rarely stand in front of a group, but rather sit around a conference table, often with a built-in projection system. In other situations, a presenter would be expected to stand in front of a group that sits in formal rows of chairs. If your team has the option to choose a delivery style, discuss how you might be most effective. Many excellent presenters feel more comfortable on their feet, since they can move around and put more physical energy into their presentations. Others might find more receptive listeners with a less formal style. Your goal for your team presentation should help to guide you in this decision.

- *Who will present this presentation?* The temptation for many teams is to select the team member who is the best speaker and nominate that person to do the entire presentation. This is, of course, one option, but it is rarely one that works best. If this is truly a team effort, the whole team should be involved in the preparation of the material, and, unless it's a very large team, all team members should speak during the presentation and/or the question-and-answer session. Even though presentation skill levels may vary considerably within your team, the expertise that each individual brings to the project can generally compensate for less-than-perfect delivery skills. Furthermore, demonstrating the commitment of all team members to the presentation can enhance team and message credibility. (See Table 21.1.)

TABLE 21.1 INTERNATIONAL TEAM MEMBERS

Some of our international students and clients have been reluctant to participate in team presentations because they feel their language skills are not good enough for an American audience. We have always encouraged these people to participate fully in their team presentations, usually with excellent results. We have found two interesting things happen:

- First, most managers and executives today are becoming familiar with Asian, European, and South American dialects because corporate culture in general is becoming so international. Once an audience becomes used to the differences in pronunciation of a speaker, it generally is not a distraction.

- Second, a business audience is there to hear the content of your message. With the exception of speech instructors or consultants, listeners are rarely there to critique a speaker's delivery skills—they want to focus on your message. Unless an individual's skills are so poor as to make him or her unintelligible, international speakers rarely present a problem for business teams.

A TEAM PRESENTATION WITHOUT A WRITTEN DOCUMENT

Obviously, if you are beginning a presentation from scratch, you will need to do a considerable amount of work in planning the presentation before you get to the aspects of team delivery described in the preceding section. We recommend that you go back to Chapters 11 to 17 and work through the seven steps in the presentation process, from defining your purpose to handling questions and answers. While some of the work may be divided among members of the team, you need to keep all team members informed and involved through each step of this process. This ensures that your presentation can be supported by everyone and that everyone can participate fully.

GENERAL GUIDELINES FOR PRESENTING AS A TEAM

- *Practice the presentation together as a team.* While you may be familiar with the material, especially if you are presenting from a team-written document, the team presentation should appear as a unified whole—not as a series of minipresentations. Additionally, practicing team presentations helps you to revisit the content of the presentation for accuracy, as well as to identify any areas of overlap or redundancy. It gives you a chance to make sure your visual aids work well from a mechanical standpoint (e.g., "Can this computer projection system read my PowerPoint disk?") as well as a visual standpoint ("Oops, the fluorescent colors really don't look too professional, do they?"). You can also use rehearsal time to help one another on delivery skills (as in, "Joe, be sure not to block the screen with your body when you show that slide.") and improve overall comfort level within the team.

- *Introduce yourself and the members of the team.* Where appropriate, provide some background on your involvement with the project. Unless you can be 100 percent sure that everyone in the room knows each presenter, this step is essential. It will establish some familiarity with the team and enhance your credibility as speakers.

- *Use the introduction to preview the content of the presentation and how the team will present it.* This preview will give your audience a framework demonstrating how you will proceed, making it easier to follow. The preview could be something as simple as this: "First, I'll be describing some background information on the project and how we approached

our study. Then Joe will described the data we collected and our forecast for the next year. Next, Mary
will discuss some of the liabilities of going along with
this project. And I'll be back at the end to talk about
some of our recommendations."

- *Plan clear transitions between speaker segments.*
  Transitions serve as signposts for your listeners so
  they can follow the presentation more easily. A common team transition is the internal summary, where
  the speaker might say something like, "Now that I
  have shown you how the data supports this project,
  I'll turn this over to Mary, who will discuss some
  concerns about liabilities."

- *Visual aids used in the presentation should all follow the same format.* Many speakers today use
  Microsoft PowerPoint, and if you do, the presentation slides should be done in a consistent template,
  as a package. We have seen teams where each
  speaker did his or her own visuals, and the results
  generally appear unprofessional and uncoordinated.
  If this is indeed a team presentation, then there
  needs to be consistency among medium, format, and
  appearance to help tie the parts of the presentation
  together.

- *All team members should be available for the
  question-and-answer session at the end of the presentation.* In addition to following the guidelines in
  Chapter 17 for handling the Q&A, the team members
  should discuss ahead of time who will handle questions in specific areas. It is helpful to have all team
  members participate in the Q&A, but they should be
  neither competing to answer questions nor reluctant
  to respond to a concern.

- *As with individual presentations, the team presentation should not drift lamely to a close at the end
  of the Q&A.* One team member should signal when
  time is up and offer an appropriate closing comment
  on behalf of the group.

END POINT

While many business professionals are still responsible
for giving individual presentations, the team presentation is becoming an important part of today's corporate
culture. Understanding how to approach the task of
working as a team and working through the steps in a
systematic way will ensure the success of your writing
and presentation projects. And while many busy executives find the time involved in teamwork can be
demanding, the results of the effort are generally
thought to be worthwhile.

The Self-Diagnostic Grammar Test

The test that follows contains common errors made by MBA candidates in a top-ranked MBA program. Some are parallel to errors revealed in a study by Leonard and Gilsdorf[1] that distracted senior business executives. Others are based on common errors cited by Charles Brusaw, et. al, in *The Business Writer's Handbook.*[2]

We want to give special acknowledgment to Ms. Tammany Kramer, Ph.D. candidate in English, University of Rochester, for her assistance in developing and editing these items and the answer key.

First, circle any error in an item. (Some of the errors you circle may be legitimate grammatical errors, others may not. This will help you spot your mistakes.)

Second, correct any errors. (Think about the items in the following way: If you wouldn't sign a letter or memo with the sentence in it, you should probably change it.)

THE TEST

1. All three companies internal expenses increased dramatically during the last year.
2. The project was given to Shankar and myself for completion by Thursday.
3. Neither he nor the board members wants to schedule another Friday afternoon meeting.
4. Although the quarter's earnings fell short of projections the mood at the company was optimistic.

5. Copies of the report go to: the controller, accountant, and the CFO.

6. The consensus of opinion is that the principal affect of the buyout was to eliminate local competition.

7. She requested that the proposal be reworked to accommodate recent legislation, that was targeted at computer software companies such as ours.

8. His sales expertise is unparalled, however, his ability to maintain client relationships is quite poor.

9. Smaller than its predecessor, the design team presented a streamlined model of the new laptop.

10. An analysis of the company's industry position revealed three shortcomings. Excessive buyer power, potential substitutes, and it cannot prevent entry from other firms.

11. According to Lupe less than 14 percent of the employees took all of their sick leave, they preferred to roll it over and add it to their vacation time.

12. While Holger has been here longer than me, my performance record speaks for itself.

13. The creation of cross functional teams are crucial for eliminating production backlog.

14. He gave a presentation on risk assessment in the conference room.

15. When a manager is faced with strife between coworkers, one can expect them to use their personal skills to smooth out the situation.

16. Mr. Li wants to look into developing new product lines, such as, computer games, accounting software and foreign language programs.

17. The changes in personnel though apparently a result of company growth makes the stockholders apprehensive.

18. I sent the blueprints over to the client's office yesterday and I expect that we will get her approval within the next two or three days unless there is a major problem with the amendments.

19. Peter Walsh the senior partner in the firm welcomes the opportunity to hire fresh talent.

20. He had looked forward to the possibility of expanding into the electronics industry now his company is in a position to do so.

21. This would provide the underwriters with loss information and will promote a more timely release of renewals.

22. Between you and I, Ms. Stern never gave us a deadline.

23. Its unclear how new sales manager will influence sales.

24. It goes without saying that we would like you to give consideration to our plans for restructuring the department.

25. Causes of the decrease in sales are: late deliveries, a shortage of salespersons, and they couldn't keep up service contracts.

26. John told Thomas that the figures from the Syracuse branch were late for two consecutive months; he thinks that the New York branches are completely incompetent.

27. Ed wanted to attend the conference, one reason was that he thought he could polish up his statistical analysis skills.

28. The proposed vertical integration, that would enable a smoother production process, might prove to be prohibitively expensive.

29. Everyone who wants to attend the luncheon needs to reserve their space by Wednesday.

30. Thank you for the opportunity to submit this bid. If you have any questions, please contact me. I will call you on November 20 to follow up on the proposal. I look forward to hearing from you.

ANSWER KEY

The following are representative answers to items in the Self-Diagnostic Test. The type of error is listed in parentheses following the item. Often there are multiple ways to correct an error. Your focus should be on whether you:

- Identified the key error in the item
- Were able to correct it
- Corrected something that was not an error
- Introduced a new error

In this answer key, specific words and punctuation marks are underlined to focus your attention on the errors and the changes recommended to correct them.

After checking your answers, review a handbook on English usage to better understand the errors that you made, or contact Ron Hein & Associates, Inc. (ronhein.com, ron@eznet.net) for information on easy-to-use, self-instructional materials that clearly explain and help you eliminate errors that you are making.

1. All three companies' internal expenses increased dramatically during the last year. (possession)

2. The project was given to Shankar and me for completion by Thursday. (personal pronouns)

3. Neither he nor the board members want to schedule another Friday afternoon meeting. (correlative conjunctions, noun-verb agreement)

4. Although the quarter's earnings fell short of projections, the mood at the company was optimistic. (commas with dependent clauses)

5. Copies of the report go to the controller, the accountant, and the CFO. (colons, parallel construction)

6. The consensus is that the principal effect of the buyout was to eliminate local competition. (redundancy, affect/effect)

7.a. She requested that the proposal be reworked to accommodate recent legislation that was targeted at computer software companies such as ours.

   b. She requested that the proposal be reworked to accommodate recent legislation targeted at computer software companies such as ours. (restrictive and nonrestrictive elements, concision)

8. His sales expertise is unparalled; however, his ability to maintain client relationships is quite poor. (commas, conjunctive adverbs, semicolons)

9.a. The design team presented a streamlined model of the new laptop, which was smaller than its predecessor.

  b. The design team presented a streamlined model of <u>the new laptop that was smaller than its predecessor</u>. **(dangling modifier)**

10. An analysis of the company's industry position revealed three <u>shortcomings: excessive</u> buyer power, potential substitutes, and <u>possible entry from other firms</u>. **(colons, sentence fragment, parallel construction)**

11.a. According to Lupe, less than 14 percent of the employees took all of their sick <u>leave; they</u> preferred to roll it over and add it to their vacation time.

  b. According to Lupe, less than 14 percent of the employees took all of their sick <u>leave. They</u> preferred to roll it over and add it to their vacation time.

  c. According to Lupe, less than 14 percent of the employees took all of their sick <u>leave because they</u> preferred to roll it over and add it to their vacation time. **(comma and introductory phrase, comma splice, causal relationship)**

12. While Holger has been here longer <u>than I</u>, my performance record speaks for itself. **(subjective case)**

13. The creation of <u>cross-functional</u> teams <u>is</u> crucial for eliminating production backlog. **(hyphen, subject-verb agreement)**

14. He gave a presentation <u>in the conference room</u> on risk assessment. **(ambiguous modifier)**

15.a. When <u>a manager</u> is faced with strife between coworkers, one can expect <u>him or her</u> to use <u>his or her</u> personal skills to smooth out the situation.

  b. When <u>managers</u> are faced with strife between coworkers, one can expect <u>them</u> to use <u>their</u> personal skills to smooth out the situation. **(noun-pronoun agreement)**

16. Mr. Li wants to look into developing new product <u>lines, such as</u> computer games, accounting software, and foreign language programs. **(commas)**

17. The <u>changes</u> in <u>personnel, though</u> apparently a result of company <u>growth, make</u> the stockholders apprehensive. **(restrictive and nonrestrictive clauses, subject-verb agreement)**

18.a. I sent the blueprints over to the client's office <u>yesterday, and I</u> expect that we will get her approval within the next two or three days unless there is a major problem with the amendments.

   b. I sent the blueprints over to the client's office <u>yesterday. I</u> expect that we will get her approval within the next two or three days unless there is a major problem with the amendments. **(comma, new sentence)**

19. Peter Walsh<u>, the senior partner in the firm,</u> welcomes the opportunity to hire fresh talent. **(appositives, commas)**

20.a. He had looked forward to the possibility of expanding into the electronics <u>industry, and now</u> his company is in a position to do so.

   b. He had looked forward to the possibility of expanding into the electronics <u>industry; now</u> his company is in a position to do so.

   c. He had looked forward to the possibility of expanding into the electronics <u>industry. Now</u> his company is in a position to do so. **(run-on sentence, comma, semicolon, new sentence)**

21.a. This <u>would</u> provide the underwriters with loss information and <u>would</u> promote a more timely release of renewals.

   b. This <u>will</u> provide the underwriters with loss information and <u>will</u> promote a more timely release of renewals. **(consistent verb tense)**

22. <u>Between you and me</u>, Ms. Stern never gave us a deadline. **(pronoun case)**

23. <u>It's</u> unclear how <u>the</u> new sales manager will influence sales. **(its versus it's, articles)**

24. We would like you to <u>consider</u> our plans for restructuring the department. **(cliché, concision)**

25.a. Causes of the decrease in sales <u>are the late deliveries, the shortage of sales staff, and the inability to keep up service contracts</u>.

   b. The decrease in sales is caused by the late deliveries, the shortage of sales staff, and the inability to keep up service contracts. **(colon, parallel construction)**

26.a. John told Thomas that the figures from the Syracuse branch were late for two consecutive months; <u>John</u> thinks <u>that New York branch</u> is incompetent.

   b. John told Thomas that the figures from the Syracuse branch were late for two consecutive

months; <u>Thomas thinks that the New York branch</u> is incompetent.
(overgeneralization, ambiguous pronoun referent)

27.a. Ed wanted to attend the <u>conference because</u> he thought he could polish up his statistical analysis skills.

b. Ed wanted to attend the <u>conference. One</u> reason was that he thought he could polish up his statistical analysis skills.
(comma, causal relationship)

28. The proposed vertical <u>integration, which</u> would enable a smoother production <u>process, might</u> prove to be prohibitively expensive.   **(restrictive and nonrestrictive clauses)**

29. <u>Everyone</u> who wants to attend the luncheon needs to reserve <u>his or her</u> space by Wednesday.
(noun-pronoun agreement)

30. Thank you for the opportunity to submit this bid. I will call you on November 20 to discuss it, but please contact me in the interim if you have any questions.   **(concision, clarity, logic)**

Guidelines for Special-Occasion Presentations

While most managers and executives spend most of their presentation time informing or persuading audiences and workgroups, there are times when you will be called upon to deliver a special-occasion presentation. These kinds of presentations include:

- Speeches of introduction
- Speeches to pay tribute or present an award
- Speeches of gratitude or to acknowledge an award
- Eulogies at funerals and memorial services
- Toasts at recognition banquets and weddings

While each of these occasions is different and special in its own right, the general guidelines for all of these presentations are the same.

1. *For special-occasion presentations, you should still go through the presentation preparation process.* (See Part 3.) The early steps are the most important—determining your purpose and analyzing your audience. You need to know these things in order to determine what kinds of remarks are appropriate for the occasion and what your audience would like and needs to hear.

2. *Your role as the speaker is to focus on two specific tasks: reflecting the tone of the occasion and making a connection with the audience.* Your remarks should appropriately reflect the feelings evoked by this occasion (for example, jubilance at a colleague receiving an award for outstanding sales performance, solemnity at the untimely death of a junior executive in a car crash). It is also your job to con-

nect the occasion to the audience, to draw them
into the spirit and feeling of the event (for example,
an amusing anecdote that reflects how this salesperson achieved her success, a few lines from a
poem that the executive kept on the wall of his
office for inspiration).

3. *Keep your remarks short.* Most special-occasion presentations should take no more than 2 to 3 minutes.
Most often, you are not the main focus of the occasion, so let your audience appreciate your remarks
as a supplement to their overall listening experience.

Here are some basic guidelines specific to each type
of special-occasion presentation.

INTRODUCTIONS

Avoid the trite, "Here's a person who needs no introduction . . ." in favor of a well-prepared and thoughtful
speech. Be sure to get some background information on
the person you will be introducing, and use that information in the most glowing terms. While light humor
may be appropriate if your speaker is somewhat
humorous or fun-loving, it is inappropriate to make fun
at the speaker's expense (unless this is a "roast"). You
don't need to give a person's complete history, but outline the points most relevant to the talk, state why the
individual is an appropriate speaker for this group, and
introduce the speaker's topic or the title of the talk.

PAYING TRIBUTE OR PRESENTING
AN AWARD

These speeches are very focused. You are there to
acknowledge the accomplishments of a colleague and
present some recognition of those accomplishments.
You should definitely gather information about the person's background as it relates to the recognition he or
she is receiving. It is also appropriate to personalize
the attributes of the award recipient for your audience,
perhaps by relating a personal experience you had
with the recipient or an anecdote related to you by a
colleague.

GIVING SPEECHES OF GRATITUDE
OR ACCEPTING AN AWARD

When you are the recipient of an award, you should
thank the group or organization sponsoring the award.
You should also thank coworkers, team members, or
even family and friends in some cases—those who supported you and made it possible for you to win this

recognition. You can also go beyond the standard thank-you remarks and share a lesson, an idea, or a brief inspirational story that will connect you with the audience.

EULOGIES AT FUNERALS AND MEMORIAL SERVICES

These can be among the most difficult presentations to plan. There is generally so much emotion involved in the death of a close family member or coworker that many find it difficult to speak publicly at these times. If you have accepted the invitation to deliver a eulogy, you should spend much of your preparation time reflecting on the deceased and on the the words that would bring most comfort to your audience. The eulogy is one place where the sincere speaker is always appreciated, even if the delivery is not the most articulate or polished.

TOASTS AT RECOGNITION BANQUETS AND WEDDINGS

Most of us have been to enough banquets and weddings to see examples of how *not* to deliver a toast. Some of the most common don'ts are as follows:

- Don't deliver a toast with no preparation: "Here's to Harry and his lovely bride what's-her-name . . ."
- Don't deliver a toast after you have been partaking of the open bar with great enthusiasm.
- Don't deliver a toast with private jokes and references that only a few people in the audience can understand. A corollary: Don't deliver a toast in a language only a few attendees can understand.

You should consider it an honor to be asked to deliver a toast, and you should put as much thought and preparation into this speech as you would other presentations.

Once again, you should think of the person or couple who is receiving the toast and the reason for the occasion. Consider the special attributes of the people involved and consider the audience and what they want to hear.

END POINT

Special-occasion presentations are often not a routine part of an executive's speaking calendar, and yet they can be significant in your personal and professional development. With the proper preparation and practice, they can become a natural part of your professional portfolio.

Sample E-mail Documents

**Sample Document #1:
Draft E-mail**

To: tom@ccnet1.net
From: ron@eznet.net
Date: January 9, 1999
Subject: hello

The audit reports for ccnet1.net are ready for your review. Please take a look at them and let us know if you have any questions or recommendations.

**Sample Document #2:
Draft E-mail with Improved Subject
Line**

To: tom@ccnet1.net
From: ron@eznet.net
Date: January 9, 1999
Subject: Please review audit reports for ccnet1.net

The audit reports for ccnet1.net are ready for your review. Please take a look at them and let us know if you have any questions or recommendations.

Sample Document #3:
Draft E-mail with Visual Cues

To: tom@ccnet1.net
From: ron@eznet.net
Date: January 9, 1999
Subject: Please review audit reports for ccnet1.net by Monday, January 11, 1999
Attachment: ccnet1-audit98.rtf

Hello Tom—

Thank you for your help on the ccnet1 audit.

Timeline. Please review the attached audit reports (ccnet1-audit98.rtf) for your company by Monday, January 11, 1999.

Process suggestions. If you have questions or recommendations for changes, please send me an e-mail with your questions and/or recommendations. Including citations with the page numbers of the audit report will help us process your questions and recommendations more efficiently.

Contact person. As we discussed, I will be the contact person for this project.

Ron Hein
Senior Auditor

ron@eznet.net
(716) 671-6170

Sample Business Letters

Before

NegotiationPRO, Inc.
San Francisco, California

January 14, 1999

> Unclear where letter is going. No visual cues.

Dear Ms. Lindsay Ayn:

> Which software?

The attached CD-ROM contains an updated version of the software (what program?) that will allow you to work with Windows 98. We apologize for the (our) delay in releasing the program and any inconvenience that it may have caused you.

> First? Beta? What does this mean to me?

This program is now compatible with Windows 98 and you to use your application (program/software) within the Windows 98 environment. However, this first version is a beta version and it does not have the toolbars found in traditional Windows programs. Nonetheless, the program functions quite well.

> 2x negative phrasing— "does not" & "Nonetheless"?

> "preliminary test version" or beta version?

This preliminary test version requires some different installation procedures (it is not self-starting from the CD-ROM). Those instructions are on the CD-ROM in the "How-to.txt" file. To install the program, open the file with any text editor and simply follow the step-by-step directions. If you require technical support, please call (701) 555-1111.

> I'm in Texas—what time zone and hours?

A complete version of the program, with the toolbars should be available in two to six weeks, and it will be available for downloading on the Internet from our web page. Starting in June of this year, a complete version of the program will also be in retail stores.

> A vague date is not helpful. Why not in retail for *six months*?

> Does customer have Internet access vs. CD?

Again, we thank you for your patience and understanding and we apologize for difficulties the delay has caused.

> Phrasing might cause liability.

Very sincerely yours,

> Overly friendly.

The Technical Department

> Writer's name/title would be a nice touch.

After

Edited for the Following Concerns:

- Brievity
- Visual cues
- Emphasis on *free*
- Organization
- Positive phrasing
- Company/software name

NegotiationPRO, Inc.
San Francisco, California

January 14, 1999

Ms. Lindsay Ayn
Purchasing Department
Ron Hein and Associates, Inc.
P. O. Box 314
Webster, New York 14580-0314

Subject: Free upgrade to NegotiationPRO 3.0

Dear Ms. Lindsay Ayn:

As a <u>free upgrade service</u> to our registered customers, we have enclosed the latest version of our Negotiation-PRO software. Version 3.0 of NegotiationPRO is designed for improved performance using Windows 98. This free upgrade is our way of apologizing for our delay in releasing the program.

<u>Features and Upgrades.</u> Version 3.0 uses all standard Windows 98 features, with the exception of toolbars. Version 3.01, which will be sent to you free in six weeks, will add the toolbars feature. Version 3.01 will also be available for downloading from our Internet site (http//:www.negotiationpro.com).

<u>Installation and Technical Services.</u> Complete installation directions for NegotiationPRO are included on the CD-ROM in the "How-to.txt" file, which can be opened by any word processing program (for example, Notepad or WordPad). If you have any questions or require technical support, please call (701) 555–1111 (Monday–Saturday, 8:00 a.m. to 8:00 p.m., Central Time) for free assistance.

Again, we thank you for your patience and understanding and for purchasing NegotiationPro, the negotiation program that helps you write winning proposals and negotiate win-win contracts.

Sincerely,

Mary Sandoval
Manager of Technical Services

Enclosure: NegotiationPRO 3.0 (CD-ROM)

Before

The Orchard Corporation
100 7th Place N.W. • Portland, Oregon
(503) 555-1212

March 30, 1999

City of Wilsontown
Planning and Zoning Board
123 State Street North
Wilsontown, Oregon xxxxx

Re: Project Site Plan
State Street and Southwest Road

Gentlemen:

> Gender-specific usage

> Unclear—who requested/purpose

Enclosed is a survey prepared by **The Orchard**. Note that of the 60 school-age children who currently go to the Arcade Station, 20% will go more frequently after the renovation. Also note that some children who do not currently go to the Arcade Station would begin to use it after the renovation; however, we do not anticipate that this increased usage will lead to any planning or zoning issues.

> Imprecise numbers

Please place this matter on the Planning and Zoning Board calendar for April 13, 1999, so that we may discuss the matter. An **Orchard Corporation** staff member will be present at that time.

Sincerely yours,

> Lack of visual cues throughout letter

Tom Hayes
Assistant Vice President for **The Orchard Corporation**

Enclosure

> Insufficient

After

Edited for the Following Concerns:

- Purpose/Request
- Visual Cues
- Gender-specific titles
- Organization
- Positive phrasing

The Orchard Corporation
100 7th Place N.W. • Portland, Oregon
(503) 555-1212

March 30, 1999

City of Wilsontown
Planning and Zoning Board
123 State Street North
Wilsontown, Oregon xxxxx

Re: Project Site Plan
State Street and Southwest Road

Dear Board Members:

We have enclosed the survey requested by the City of Wilsontown Planning and Zoning Board at your meeting on December 15, 1998. It was requested that we determine the number of school-age children who currently go to our client's location (The Arcade Station), as well as the number of children who would go after renovation of the business.

Our Findings. Based upon a random survey of 207 families with school-age children, we found that of the 60 school-age children who currently go to the Arcade Station, 20% will go more frequently after the renovation and 41 others will go for the first time. We do not anticipate that this increased usage will lead to any planning or zoning issues.

Requested Action. Please place this matter on the Planning and Zoning Board calendar for April 13, 1999 so that we may discuss the matter. As requested, an **Orchard Corporation** staff member will be present at that time to address any questions.

Sincerely,

Tom Hayes
Assistant Vice President for **The Orchard Corporation**

Enclosure: The Arcade Station Survey

Before

The FireAnts ServiceCorp
200 Third Avenue • New York City 10158

July 15, 2000

Ron Hein & Associates, Inc.
Mr. Ron Hein
P.O. Box 314
Webster, New York 14580-0314

Dear Mr. Hein:

> Instructive first sentence.

We are in the process of updating our list of writing
and editing firms. If you wish to remain on our list,
please indicate so at the bottom of this letter. A
postage-paid return envelope is enclosed for your convenience.

> Unclear if should return if
> do not want to be listed.

We cannot guarantee that your firm will
be asked to bid on (writing and editing) projects with
our company, however, your company's name and qualifications will continue to be provided on our internal
referral list for managers who might have need for your
services.

> Don't know what you
> have on your database.

If your firm has expanded its areas of
expertise since your initial contact with us, note that on
the bottom of the letter also. Thank you for your
response.

Sincerely,

Mary Elisa Bridgestone
Assistant to Van Thomas Webster

Enclosure: PPRE

☐ I wish to have my firm remain on your list
☐ Please remove my firm's name from the list

> Checklist here *helps* to get back original
> data and enter data/changes.

After

Edited for the Following Concerns:
- Organization
- Checklist of expertise
- Use of bulleted lists

The FireAnts ServiceCorp
200 Third Avenue ▪ New York City 10158

July 15, 2000

Ron Hein and Associates, Inc.
Mr. Ron Hein
P. O. Box 314
Webster, New York 14580-0314

Dear Mr. Hein:

We are in the process of updating our list of writing and editing firms. At the bottom of this letter we have listed the areas of expertise that are shown in our database for your firm. If you wish to remain on our list of service providers, please verfy and update your areas of expertise. Although we cannot guarantee that your firm will be asked to bid on projects with our company, we will keep your company's name and qualifications on our internal referral list for managers who might have need for your services.

If you do not wish to remain on our list, please check the appropriate box so that we can remove your name from our mailing lists.

A postage-paid envelope is enclosed for your convenience. Thank you for your response.

Sincerely,

Mary Elisa Bridgestone
Assistant to Van Thomas Webster

Enclosure: Return Envelope

☐ **I wish to have my firm remain on your list** (for the following areas of expertise)

- Writing-and-editing services
  Reports
  Proposals and RFPs
  Training and instructional manuals

- Training
  Improving management communication
  Developing writing and editing skills and processes
  Improving internal and external documents
  Outplacement (resumes and cover letters)

- Other (list):

☐ **Please remove my firm's name from the list**

E

Proposals and Requests for Proposals

SAMPLE LETTER FOR REQUEST
FOR A PROPOSAL

WICS, Incorporated

10000 Peach Tree Blvd, Suite 1001 • Atlanta, Georgia
100 Avenue of the Americas, 15th Floor • New York City, New York
(212) 555-1212 • wics3.com

October 31, 1999

Ms. Labanowski
SouthEASTERN Inventory Systems
1500 Rundell Road
Marrietta, Georgia

Request for Proposals: Warehouse Inventory Control
System 3 (**WICS3**)

Dear Ms. Labanowski:

Your company requested proposal specifications for the
Warehouse Inventory Control System 3 (WICS3) that we
need to have designed and built at our Atlanta location.
Previously, you received the Project Requirements; we
have attached the Proposal Specifications to this letter.

- Project Requirements:
    General instructions to bidders
    Draft or proposed contract and schedule
    Statement of the requirements/work
- Proposal Specifications:
    Technical Strategy
    Management Strategy
    Cost Strategy

Please note that we reserve the right to reject

- Proposals that do not follow our proposal
  specifications
- Proposals from unqualified bidders
- Proposals received after January 10, 2001, 5:00 p.m.
  EST

If we can be of assistance to you during your proposal
preparation process, with either requirement or specifi-
cation information, please contact

    Mr. Isamu Hitachi
    Technical Manager
    WICS3 Proposal Management Team
    Phone: (212) 555-1212
    Fax: (212) 555-1212
    E-mail: isamu@wics3.com

We look forward to receiving your proposal.

Sincerely,

Reba F. T. Morgan
Project Manager, **WICS3**

Attachment: **WICS3** Proposal Specifications

SAMPLE PROPOSAL SPECIFICATIONS

RFP Release Date: October 21, 1999
Proposal Due Date: January 10, 2001, 5:00 p.m. EST

Contact/Information:

Mr. Isamu Hitachi
Technical Manager
WICS3 Proposal Management Team
Phone: (212) 555-1212
Fax: (212) 555-1212
E-mail: isamu@wics3.com

To facilitate our evaluation process, please arrange the content of your proposal for the Warehouse Inventory Control System (WICS3) in the following sequence. Please submit in it in hardcopy and as Word 97 (.rtf) and Excel files.

1. Technical Strategy
   - Your company's understanding of the problem(s)
   - How your company will solve the problem(s)
   - Why your company's solution will work
   - The nature of your company's "product" or solution
   - Your schedule and completion date, including when "A" starts/ends; when "B" starts/ends; etc.

2. Management Strategy
   - How you can carry out the solution
     - Relevant Experience, client list (last 5 years), historical success, insights gained
     - Personnel (with resumes)
     - Internal organization
     - Facilities
     - Outside resources (needed/available)
     - Company financial statements (prior 5 years) and banking references
     - Quality control mechanisms

3. Cost Strategy
   - Why your solution is affordable
   - Why your proposal is reasonable and competitive
   - The direct and indirect benefits of working with your company
   - Spreadsheets (Excel) showing your budget/costs arranged by
     - RFP/IFB requirements
     - Category (personnel/supplies/equipment/facilities)
     - Benefit
     - Fiscal periods/project phases

Sample Report

NANO TECHNOLOGIES: A PRELIMINARY COST-BENEFIT ANALYSIS PROJECT B-1999-07

Recommendation. Based upon the attached analysis and noted assumptions, we recommend entering into a contract to produce a book using our group's technical knowledge of nano technologies (MEMS—Microelectromechanical systems) and the writers/content experts from *Option B* (details below).

Value/Benefits. There are three primary benefits to completing the proposed contract:

- Value of the book as a marketing tool
- Development of publication skills and processes of specific employees
- Modest profit (loss) potential (dependent upon chosen writers/content experts)

Assumptions. Our analysis of this project is complex in that we need to make a series of related assumptions on benefits (profit, marketing/advertising value, skill/process development, and costs), using projections for revenue (Table 1) and cost/salary (Table 2).

Benefit Assumptions and Calculations. We project three benefits (profit + marketing value + publication skills and process development). Any potential for a (loss) can be controlled.

1. Profit (Profit = revenue – costs). We have calculated a profit (loss) range varying dependent upon total

sales and salary costs for the two writers/content experts. We have estimated the number of hours specific tasks will require (Table 2) to determine the primary costs associated with the project and have compared those costs with the projected revenues (Table 1).

These calculations are based upon revenue projections ranging from $10,000 (advance only) to $85,000 (advance plus 100,000 sales yielding 10% of the wholesale price, $7.50), less the primary cost, the writer's salaries projected to range from $23,125 to $96,475 depending upon the per hour salary burden of individual writers ($25/hr to $150/hr).

We have writers/content experts available who have the content expertise and writing ability to complete the project for $25/hour to $150/hour (resumes and confidential salary information are available). The two identified writers/content experts in the $45/hour range have excellent skills and knowledge (Option B).

TABLE 1 REVENUE PROJECTION FOR PROJECT B-1999-07 (NEGOTIATED CONTRACT)

Sales/Year	1,000	5,000	10,000	20,000	
(Commission 7.5%)					
Year 1	$ 560	$2,750	$5,600	$11,200	
Year 2	$ 560	$2,750	$5,600	$11,200	
Year 3	$ 560	$2,750	$5,600	$11,200	
Year 4	$ 560	$2,750	$5,600	$11,200	
Year 5	$ 560	$2,750	$5,600	$11,200	
Range	$2800			$56,000	$ 2,800–$56,000
Total Revenue Potential @ 7.5% with $10,000 Advance (0 to 100,000 sales)					$12,800–$56,000
Total with advance; minimal-maximum sales @ 7.5%					
(Commission 10%)					
Year 1	$ 750	$3750	$7500	$15,000	
Year 2	$ 750	$3750	$7500	$15,000	
Year 3	$ 750	$3750	$7500	$15,000	
Year 4	$ 750	$3750	$7500	$15,000	
Year 5	$ 750	$3750	$7500	$15,000	
Range	$3750			$75,000	$ 3,750–$75,000
Total Revenue Potential @ 10% with $10,000 Advance (0 to 100,000 sales)					$13,750–$85,000

Option A: Using the two writers/content experts in the $25/hour range ($23,125) produces the best scenario for generating a profit over 5 years, including discounting all fixed costs. However, this option is *not recommended* due to the high probability of needing additional content expertise and creating increased workloads for others throughout the organization. Profit/(loss) @ $25/hr: ($13,125) to $68,875

☑ *Option B.* Using two writers/content experts in the $45/hour ($46,250) range would provide the most realistic scenarios for generating a profit over 5 years, including discounting all fixed costs. If the project is pursued, Option B is *recommended.* Profit/(loss) @ $45/hr: ($36,250) to $38,750

Option C. Using two writers/content experts in the $75/hour range ($64,250) is *not recommended* due to workload. They would be available on a support basis, with minimal cost impact. Profit/(loss) @ $75/hr: ($54,250) to $20,750

Option D. Using two writers/content experts in the $100/hour range ($82,500) is *not recommended* due to workload and writing skills. They would be available on a support basis, with minimal cost impact. Profit/(loss) @ $100/hr: ($72,500) to $2,500

Option E. Using two writers/content experts in the $150/hour range ($96,475) would lead to a loss on the project, even discounting all fixed costs, and is *not recommended* due to more appropriate uses of the individuals' time. They could be listed as coauthors to increase recognition, and improve marketing and advertising options. Profit/(loss) @ $150/hr: ($86,475) to ($11,475)

2. Marketing value. Potential advertising/marketing uses would include (publisher advertising, seminars-linkages, web site usage), and can be increased by listing specific senior executives as coauthors (see Option E, above). To ensure a conservative estimate of the value of the project, no dollar value is projected for this benefit.

3. Skill/process development. There is strong potential for improvement in the writing/editing skill levels of individual contributors and the group, as well as improving knowledge of the publishing process. These improved skills would have value for future projects and would decrease the costs associated with training seminars. To ensure a conservative estimate of the value of the project, no dollar value is projected for this benefit.

Basis of Calculations. The potential profit for the project is summarized using the data in Table 1 (Revenue) and Table 2 (Cost, salaries).

A. Profit. The potential profit for this project is defined as revenue minus costs.

> Revenue—The revenue potential of the project is defined by a negotiated contract, which is summarized in (Table 1: Revenue Projection for Project B-1999-07).
>
> Costs—Four cost factors were evaluated.
>
>> Fixed costs. The primary fixed cost is a salary line for the potential writers/experts (Table 2). This salary line is calculated across a range of hourly rates ($25–$150/hour). Other fixed costs are neutral (i.e., facilities, equipment, support staff) with respect to the project.
>>
>> Potential lost revenue. It is assumed that the potential loss of revenue associated with individual contributors (writers) due to their association will be minimal due to the use of contract writers. In fact, the use of contract writers to replace our writers who will be on this project will give us a low-risk opportunity to explore alternative staffing options.
>>
>> Workload. The workloads of the individual contributors will remain constant, as the writers will be released from participation in other projects (replaced by contract employees, see Table 2), and the facilities, support staff costs, etc., are sunk costs.
>>
>> Potential liabilities. The potential liabilities associated with the project are minimal, and using an appropriate postwriting process will allow us to validate the lack of liability.

B. Marketing value. There are several marketing and/or advertising uses for the project; however associating cost/benefit values with them is problematic. The key value is an opportunity to leverage the company's image and increase consulting (seminar, etc.) work. No dollar value is assigned to this opportunity.

C. Skill/process development. Two potential added benefits from involvement in the project. The first is the potential for skill development of individual writers (their ability to handle materials written for external publication rather than for the internal use of corporate clients). We can subsequently leverage this skill in two ways: negotiating contracts for other publications based upon internally held knowledge, and/or selling/vending those skills to clients who need to publish materials.

TABLE 2 SALARY RANGES (TASK/HOURS × HOURLY RATE) FOR POTENTIAL CONTRIBUTORS FOR PROJECT B-1999-07

Task	Hours	$25/hr	$35	$50	$75	$100	$150
1) Lost Income							
a) Submitting	50	$1250	$1750	$2500	$3750	$5000	$7500
b) Negotiating contract (with legal)	25	$625	$875	$1250	$1750	$2500	$3750
c) Research time (10–15 hrs./chapters)	150	$3750	$5250	$7500	$11250	$15000	$22500
d) Drafting time (5 = 75/15 chapters)	75	$375	$525	$750	$1125	$1500	$2250
e) Editing time (3×, 10/per edit)	30	$750	$1050	$1500	$2250	$3000	$4500
f) Figures/tables (3×, 3.3/3 = 10/15 chapters)	150	$3750	$5250	$7500	$11250	$15000	$22500
g) Sample materials (2-8 × 2.5 or 2/10)	5	$125	$150	$250	$375	$500	$750
	20	$500	$700	$1000	$1500	$2000	$3000
h) Working with colleague (5, 15)	75	$1875	$2625	$3750	$5625	$7500	$11250
i) Working with series editor (2, 15)	30	$750	$1050	$1500	$2250	$3000	$4500
j) Proofing after copy editor (5, 15)	75	$1875	$2625	$3750	$5625	$7500	$11250
j) General clean up of chapters (2, 15)	30	$750	$1050	$1500	$2250	$3000	$4500
2) Training replacement editors (10–20 hrs/2)	20	$500	$700	$1000	$1000	$1000	$1000
	40	$1000	$1400	$2000	$2000	$2000	$2000
3) Replacement editors ($25–$50/hr = 15/wk/12)	180	$4500	$6300	$9000	$9000	$9000	$9000
4) Tracking projects (time, 1–2 hr/day/90)	90	$2250	$3150	$4500	$6750	$9000	$13500
	180	$4500	$6300	$9000	$13500	$18000	$27000
5) Total Projected Salary Ranges		$23125	$32350	$46250	$64250	$82500	$96475

Hourly Rate

Next Steps. There are four possible courses of action. The first two options are for us to notify the publisher that the project is not profitable as proposed and to (a) decline to participate or (b) negotiate further. A third option is to locate an alternate publisher. A fourth option is to proceed and use the project as a marketing tool. We *recommend* proceeding and using the project as a marketing tool by listing senior executives as co-authors.

INTRODUCTION

1. Fisher, Anne. "The High Cost of Living and Not Writing Well." *Fortune,* December 7, 1998, p. 244.
2. "Communication and teamwork." *SIAM Report on Mathematics in Industry.* This report can be accessed through the web site for the Society for Industrial and Applied Mathematics at www.siam.org/mii/node26.html.

CHAPTER 1

1. Deming, W. Edwards. *Out of the Crisis.* Cambridge, Massachusetts: MIT, 1982.
2. Camp, Robert C. *Benchmarking.* Milwaukee: ASQC/American Society for Quality Control, 1989.
3. Camp, Robert C. *Business Process Benchmarking.* Milwaukee: ASQC/American Society for Quality Control, 1995.
4. Russell, A. William. *CIRM Logistics (Certified Integrated Resource Management).* Falls Church, Virginia: APICS/American Production and Inventory Control Society, 1991.
5. Kayser, Thomas. *Mining Group Gold.* El Segundo, California: Serif Publishing, 1990.
6. Hammer, Michael, and James Champy. *Reengineering the Corporation.* New York City: Harper-Business, 1993.
7. Drucker, Peter. "The Emerging Theory of Manufacturing." *Harvard Business Review,* May–June 1990.
8. Covey, Stephen R. *Principle-Centered Leadership.* New York City: Simon & Schuster, 1991.
9. Fisher, Roger, William Ury, and Bruce Patton. *Getting to Yes,* second edition (The Harvard Negotiation Project). New York City: Penguin, 1991.

CHAPTER 3

1. Brusaw, Charles T., Gerald J. Alred, and Walter E. Oliu. *The Business Writer's Handbook,* fourth edition. New York City: St. Martin's Press, 1993.
2. Ruch, William V., and Maurice L. Crawford. *Business Reports: Oral and Written.* Boston: PWS-Kent, 1988.

CHAPTER 4

1. Penrose, John M. Jr., Robert W. Rasberry, and Robert J. Myers. *Advanced Business Communication.* Boston: PWS-Kent, 1990.
2. Sterkel, Karen S. *Effective Business and Professional Letters.* Reston, Virginia: Reston Publishing/Prentice-Hall, 1983.

CHAPTER 5

1. *The Chicago Manual of Style,* fourteenth edition. Chicago: University of Chicago Press, 1993.
2. DeVries, Mary A. *Prentice Hall Style Manual.* Englewood Cliffs, New Jersey: Prentice Hall, 1992.
3. *Publication Manual of the American Psychological Association,* fourth edition. Washington, D.C.: American Psychological Association, 1994.
4. Jordan, Lewis, editor. *The New York Times Manual of Style and Usage,* revised. New York City: Times Books, 1976.
5. Sabin, William A. *The Gregg Reference Manual,* seventh edition. New York: Glencoe, Macmillan/McGraw-Hill, 1994.

CHAPTER 6

1. http://emailhelp.com/email-ed.html.

CHAPTER 7

1. Brusaw, Charles T., Gerald J. Alred, and Walter E. Oliu. *The Business Writer's Handbook,* fourth edition. New York City: St. Martin's Press, 1993.
2. Forbes, Malcolm. "How to Write a Business Letter." In Harty, Kevin J., editor, *Strategies for Business and Technical Writing,* third edition. New York City: Harcourt Brace Jovanovich, 1989.

CHAPTER 8

1. Sabin, William A. *The Gregg Reference Manual,* seventh edition. New York City: Glencoe, Macmillan/McGraw-Hill, 1994.
2. DeVries, Mary A. *Prentice Hall Style Manual.* Englewood Cliffs, New Jersey: Prentice Hall, 1992.
3. Forbes, Malcolm. "How to Write a Business Letter." In Harty, Kevin J., editor, *Strategies for Business and Technical Writing,* third edition. New York City: Harcourt Brace Jovanovich, 1989.
4. Gelderman, Carol. "Business Letters." In DiGaetani, John L., editor, *The Handbook of Executive Communication.* Homewood, Illinois: Dow Jones-Irwin, 1986.
5. Jordan, Lewis, editor. *The New York Times Manual of Style and Usage,* revised. New York City: Times Books, 1976.

6. *The Chicago Manual of Style,* fourteenth edition. Chicago: University of Chicago Press, 1993.

CHAPTER 9

1. Vinci, Vincent. "Ten Report Writing Pitfalls: How to Avoid Them." In Harty, Kevin J., editor, *Strategies for Business and Technical Writing,* third edition. New York City: Harcourt Brace Jovanovich, 1989.
2. Brown, Leland. *Effective Business Report Writing,* fourth edition. Englewood Cliffs, New Jersey: Prentice-Hall, 1985.
3. Bowman, Joel P., and Bernadine P. Branchaw. *Business Report Writing,* second edition. New York City: Dryden Press/Holt, Rinehart and Winston, 1988.
4. Brusaw, Charles T., Gerald J. Alred, and Walter E. Oliu. *The Business Writer's Handbook,* fourth edition. New York City: St. Martin's Press, 1993.

CHAPTER 10

1. Stewart, Rodney D., and Ann L. Stewart. *Proposal Preparation,* second edition. New York City: Wiley-Interscience, 1992.
2. Fisher, Roger, William Ury, and Bruce Patton. *Getting to Yes,* second edition (The Harvard Negotiation Project). New York City: Penguin, 1991.
3. Penrose, John M. Jr., Robert W. Rasberry, and Robert J. Myers. *Advanced Business Communication.* Boston: PWS-Kent, 1990.

PART 3 INTRODUCTION

1. See, for example: James Belohlov, Paul Popp, and Michael Port, "Communication: A View from the Inside of Business," *Journal of Business Communication* (November 1974), pp. 53–59; Dan B. Curtis, Jerry L. Winsor, and Ronald D. Stephens, "National Preferences in Business and Communication Education," *Communication Education* 38 (January 1989), p. 11; Richard Nelson Bolles, *What Color Is Your Parachute? A Practical Manual for Job Hunters and Career Changers* (Berkeley, California: Ten Speed Press, 1998).

CHAPTER 15

1. "I Dug Your Laser Light Show, But . . ." *Presentations,* October 1998, p. 15.
2. Skopec, Eric W. *Business and Professional Speaking.* Englewood Cliffs, New Jersey: Prentice-Hall, 1983, p. 35.

CHAPTER 16

1. Skopec, Eric W. *Business and Professional Speaking.* Englewood Cliffs, New Jersey: Prentice-Hall, 1983, pp. 94–95.

APPENDIX A

1. Leonard, Donald J., and Jeanette W. Gilsdorf. "Language in Change: Academics' and Executives' Perceptions of Usage Errors." *The Journal of Business Communication,* spring 1990, 27(2), pp. 137–158.
2. Brusaw, Charles T., Gerald J. Alred, and Walter E. Oliu. *The Business Writer's Handbook,* fourth edition. New York City: St. Martin's Press, 1993.

BUSINESS STRATEGY AND COMMUNICATION

Camp, Robert C. *Benchmarking.* Milwaukee: ASQC/American Society for Quality Control, 1989.

Camp, Robert C. *Business Process Benchmarking.* Milwaukee: ASQC/American Society for Quality Control, 1995.

Covey, Stephen R. *Principle-Centered Leadership.* New York: Simon & Schuster, 1991.

Deming, W. Edwards. *Out of the Crisis.* Cambridge, Massachusetts: MIT, 1982.

Drucker, Peter. "The Emerging Theory of Manufacturing." *Harvard Business Review,* May–June 1990.

Fisher, Roger, William Ury, and Bruce Patton. *Getting to Yes,* second edition (The Harvard Negotiation Project). New York: Penguin, 1991.

Hammer, Michael, and James Champy. *Reengineering the Corporation.* New York: HarperBusiness, 1993.

Kayser, Thomas. *Mining Group Gold.* El Segundo, California: Serif Publishing, 1990.

Russell, A. William. *CIRM Logistics* (Certified Integrated Resource Management). Falls Church, Virginia: APICS/American Production and Inventory Control Society, 1991.

GRAMMAR, ENGLISH USAGE, AND STYLE

Broadview Book of Common Errors in English. Lewiston, New York: Broadway Press, 1988.

The Chicago Manual of Style, fourteenth edition. Chicago: University of Chicago Press, 1993.
   Over 900 pages of the best style information in print, production, printing, bookmaking.

Corder, Jim W., and John L. Ruszkiewicz. *Handbook of Current English,* eighth edition. Glenview, Illinois: Scott, Foresman, 1989.

DeVries, Mary A. *Prentice Hall Style Manual.* Englewood Cliffs, New Jersey: Prentice Hall, 1992.
Almost 500 pages of style, preparation, letters, memos, usage.

Gefvert, Constance. *The Confident Writer: A Norton Handbook.* New York City: Norton, 1988.

Jordan, Lewis, editor. *The New York Times Manual of Style and Usage,* revised. New York City: Times Books, 1976.

Pearlmann, Daniel D., and Paula R. Pearlmann. *Guide to Rapid Revision,* fourth edition. New York: Macmillan, 1989.

Pearlmann, Daniel D. *Letter Perfect: ABC for Business.* New York City: Macmillan, 1985.

Publication Manual of the American Psychological Association, fourth edition. Washington, D.C.: American Psychological Association, 1994.

Sabin, William A. *The Gregg Reference Manual,* seventh edition. New York: Glencoe, Macmillan/ McGraw-Hill, 1994.
Excellent grammar, usage, and style information.

Strunk, William Jr., and E. B. White. *The Elements of Style,* third edition. New York City: Macmillan, 1979.

Words into Type, third edition. Englewood Cliffs, New Jersey: Prentice-Hall, 1974.

LETTERS AND MEMOS

DiGaetani, John L., editor. *The Handbook of Executive Communication.* Homewood, Illinois: Dow Jones-Irwin, 1986.
Strong collection of articles, general principles of writing and speaking (894 pages).

Easton, Thomas E. "Passing the Conversational Test." In DiGaetani, John L., editor, *The Handbook of Executive Communication.* Homewood, Illinois: Dow Jones-Irwin, 1986.

Fielden, John S. "What Do You Mean You Don't Like My Style?" In Harty, Kevin J., editor, *Strategies for Business and Technical Writing,* third edition. New York: Harcourt Brace Jovanovich, 1989.

Forbes, Malcolm. "How to Write a Business Letter." In Harty, Kevin J., editor, *Strategies for Business and Technical Writing,* third edition. New York: Harcourt Brace Jovanovich, 1989.

Gelderman, Carol. "Business Letters." In DiGaetani, John L., editor, *The Handbook of Executive Commu-*

nication. Homewood, Illinois: Dow Jones-Irwin, 1986.

Guenther, Barbara. "Managerial Tact." In DiGaetani, John L., editor, *The Handbook of Executive Communication.* Homewood, Illinois: Dow Jones-Irwin, 1986.

Pharris, Joyce. "How Well Can MBAs Write?" *Stanford Business School Magazine,* fall 1987, pp. 20–23.

Sterkel, Karen S. *Effective Business and Professional Letters.* Reston, Virginia: Reston Publishing/Prentice-Hall, 1983.
> Excellent ideas, examples, common problems, good appendixes (177 pages).

VanHuss, Susie H. *Basic Letter and Memo Writing,* second edition. Cincinnati, Ohio: South-Western Publishing, 1987.
> Workbook approach, 10 guides for better writing, good sample letters (202 pages).

Wells, Patricia. "Memos That Work." In DiGaetani, John L., editor. *The Handbook of Executive Communication.* Homewood, Illinois: Dow Jones-Irwin, 1986.

PROPOSALS

Halpern, Jeanne W., Judith M. Kilborn, and Agnes M. Lokke. *Business Writing Strategies and Samples.* New York: Macmillan, 1986.
> Good examples, templates for proposals.

Meador, Roy. *Guidelines for Preparing Proposals.* Chelsea, Michigan: Lewis, 1985.
> Grants, government, R&D, good tips, examples (116 pages).

Pauley, Steven E., and Daniel G. Riordan. *Technical Report Writing Today,* fourth edition. Boston: Houghton Mifflin, 1990.
> Thoughtful information, chapter on proposals.

Penrose, John M. Jr., Robert W. Rasberry, and Robert J. Myers. *Advanced Business Communication.* Boston: PWS-Kent, 1990.
> Good information and examples on internal and external proposals.

Pfeiffer, William S. *Proposal Writing: The Art of Friendly Persuasion.* Columbus, Ohio: Merrill Publishing, 1989.
> General information, selling approach (230 pages).

Stewart, Rodney D., and Ann L. Stewart. *Proposal Preparation,* second edition. New York City: Wiley-Interscience, 1992.
> Over 350 pages of excellent process steps, outlines, bids, proposals, RFPs.

REPORTS

Blicq, Ron S. *Guidelines for Report Writing,* second edition. Scarborough, Ontario: Prentice-Hall, 1990.
    Basic information, pyramid method (229 pages).

Bowman, Joel P., and Bernadine P. Branchaw. *Business Report Writing,* second edition. New York: Dryden Press/Holt, Rinehart and Winston, 1988.
    Over 600 pages of good examples and good process information.

Brown, Leland. *Effective Business Report Writing,* fourth edition. Englewood Cliffs, New Jersey: Prentice-Hall, 1985.
    Over 400 pages of rhetoric, logic, short report formats. Strong on writing/editing/revising.

Pauley, Steven E., and Daniel G. Riordan. *Technical Report Writing Today,* fourth edition. Boston: Houghton Mifflin, 1990.
    Thoughtful information, good visuals (481 pages).

Ruch, William V., and Maurice L. Crawford. *Business Reports: Oral and Written.* Boston: PWS-Kent, 1988.
    Good basic ideas (388 pages).

Vinci, Vincent. "Ten Report Writing Pitfalls: How to Avoid Them. In Harty, Kevin J., editor, *Strategies for Business and Technical Writing,* third edition. New York: Harcourt Brace Jovanovich, 1989.
    Good chapter on problem identification.

VISUALS AND GRAPHICS

Brusaw, Charles T., Gerald J. Alred, and Walter E. Oliu. *Handbook of Technical Writing,* third edition. New York: St. Martin's Press, 1987.

Golen, Steven P., and Gavin L. Ellzey. "Using Graphics in Writing." In DiGaetani, John L., editor, *The Handbook of Executive Communication.* Homewood, Illinois: Dow Jones-Irwin, 1986.

Stein, Judith K. "Presentation Visuals." In DiGaetani, John L., editor, *The Handbook of Executive Communication.* Homewood, Illinois: Dow Jones-Irwin, 1986.

Williams, Alfred B. "Using Media for a Presentation." In DiGaetani, John L., editor, *The Handbook of Executive Communication.* Homewood, Illinois: Dow Jones-Irwin, 1986.

WRITING AND EDITING PROCESSES

Bailey, Edward P. Jr. *The Plain English Approach to Business Writing.* New York City: Oxford University Press, 1990.
    Writing, clarity, style, voice, process, good information (110 pages).

Brusaw, Charles T., Gerald J. Alred, and Walter E. Oliu. *The Business Writer's Handbook,* fourth edition. New York: St. Martin's Press, 1993.
   Good examples, memos, letters, reports, proposals, grammar (784 pages).

Brusaw, Charles T., Gerald J. Alred, and Walter E. Oliu. *Handbook of Technical Writing, third edition.* New York: St. Martin's Press, 1987.
   Duplicate of *Business Writer's Handbook* with more report-writing detail (787 pages).

DiGaetani, John L., editor. *The Handbook of Executive Communication.* Homewood, Illinois: Dow Jones-Irwin, 1986.
   Strong collection of articles on general principles of writing and speaking (894 pages).

Griffin, C. W. *Writing: A Guide for Business Professionals.* New York: Harcourt Brace Jovanovich, 1987.
   Textbook style, process, letters, memos, resumes, reports, conventions (419 pages).

Halpern, Jeanne W., Judith M. Kilborn, and Agnes M. Lokke. *Business Writing Strategies and Samples.* New York: Macmillan, 1986.
   Samples, templates, letters, reports, employment communication (584 pages).

Harty, Kevin J., editor. *Strategies for Business and Technical Writing,* third edition. New York: Harcourt Brace Jovanovich, 1989.
   Good articles, process, memos, letters, reports, style, persuasion (306 pages).

Harty, Kevin J., and John Keenan. *Writing for Business and Industry: Process and Product.* New York: Macmillan, 1987.
   Text approach, good information on all topics, "PAEFO" approach (354 pages).

Henze, Geraldine. *From Murk to Masterpiece.* Homewood, Illinois: Richard D. Irwin, 1984.
   Over 100 pages; can be read and understood in three hours; improve sloppy writing styles.

Holcombe, Marya W., and Judith K. Stein. *Writing for Decision Makers,* second edition. New York: Van Nostrand Reinhold, 1987.

Leonard, Donald J., and Jeanette W. Gilsdorf. "Language in Change: Academics' and Executives' Perceptions of Usage Errors." *The Journal of Business Communication,* spring 1990, 27(2), pp. 137–158.

Pearlmann, Daniel D., and Paula R. Pearlmann. *Guide to Rapid Revision,* fourth edition. New York: Macmillan, 1989.
   Common writing errors and techniques for improving writing (105 pages).

Penrose, John M. Jr., Robert W. Rasberry, and Robert J. Myers. *Advanced Business Communication.* Boston: PWS-Kent, 1990.

Text approach, direct and indirect, persuasive messages, presentations (379 pages).

Raimes, Ann. *Keys for Writers.* Boston: Houghton Mifflin, 1996.

Excellent organization, handbook, style, format, ESL, punctuation (400 pages).

Index